A gift for:

From:

DVNEL

Forever in Love

I am my beloved's,
and my beloved is mine.

Song of Solomon 6:3

THOMAS NELSON
Since 1798

NASHVILLE   DALLAS   MEXICO CITY   RIO DE JANEIRO

Published in Nashville, Tennessee, by Thomas Nelson®. Thomas Nelson is a registered trademark of Thomas Nelson, Inc.

Thomas Nelson, Inc., titles may be purchased in bulk for educational, business, fund-raising, or sales promotional use. For information, please e-mail SpecialMarkets@ThomasNelson.com.

ISBN: 978-1-4003-1955-8

Printed in China

11 12 13 14 15 WAI 5 4 3 2 1

Contents

Learning to Love   1

Growing Together   27

Comforting Each Other   55

Accepting One Another   87

Being Companions   117

Working Together   147

Being Known   177

Living with Hope   207

Facing Hard Times   237

Growing with God   267

Rejoicing in Abundance   297

Building a Family   327

Learning
to Love

Gold

All of the gold and silver in the world is not worth as much as the abiding true love of another. Give your love as a precious gift to a mate worthy of your care and affection.

Though you lie down among the
sheepfolds, you will be like the wings
of a dove covered with silver, and
her feathers with yellow gold.

Psalm 68:13

Trust

*L*et your mate know that he or she can trust in your loyalty and fidelity. Trust is one key to a happy bonding of your love. Cultivate trust, and you cultivate a fulfilling and refreshing love life.

The heart of her husband safely trusts her;
so he will have no lack of gain.

Proverbs 31:11

Homage

Paying homage will bring the shine of love to your mate's eyes. Don't be hesitant to tell of the beauty that is brought to your life by your beloved. Take every opportunity to compliment your loved one.

My darling, you are beautiful!
Oh, you are beautiful,
and your eyes are like doves.

Song of Solomon 1:15 ɴᴄᴠ

Honeycomb

Don't withhold the sweetness of love from your spouse. Accept the delights of love with an open hand. Enjoy and rejoice in the pleasures God has ordained in marriage.

My child, eat honey because
it is good. Honey from the
honeycomb tastes sweet.

Proverbs 24:13 NCV

Virtue

irtue is the foundation of a solid marriage. Let your mate know that he or she can safely trust his or her affection and love to you. Don't give in to the temptation to squander your love in adultery.

Who can find a virtuous wife?
For her worth is far above rubies.

Proverbs 31:10

Wandering

An affair begins with the eyes. Be careful not to let your eyes deceive you. The one you desire may look very attractive, but adultery results in ugly arguments, guilt, and devastation. What looks pleasant will turn sour and destroy.

Better is the sight of the eyes than the wandering of desire. This also is vanity and grasping for the wind.

Ecclesiastes 6:9

Garden

*L*ove is like a garden. The seed of love is planted, but unless someone tends the garden, a strong plant will never grow. Love requires long, hard work. Today is a good day to start paying attention to your beloved.

Awake, O north wind, and come,
O south! Blow upon my garden,
that its spices may flow out. Let
my beloved come to his garden
and eat its pleasant fruits.

Song of Solomon 4:16

Words

Words can build a relationship or destroy it. Let your words be those that build honesty and love between you and your beloved. Speak from your heart, and your love will be healthier for it.

Pleasant words are like a honeycomb, sweetness to the soul and health to the bones.

Proverbs 16:24

Nighttime

*M*ay your nights be filled with the comfort of a binding love. Don't let the troubles of your day intrude upon the coziness of a night spent in the arms of your beloved.

Come, let us take our fill
of love until morning;
let us delight ourselves with love.

Proverbs 7:18

A Seal

*L*ove needs a seal set upon it. A seal says this love of yours is important to you. It says you will be true and faithful to your beloved. Love your mate with confidence.

Set me as a seal upon your heart,
as a seal upon your arm;
for love is as strong as death.

Song of Solomon 8:6

Act Kindly

*K*indness builds love. Act toward your beloved in a kindly manner that seeks the good of the one you love. Show your love by thinking of your mate first—before yourself. You will find a reward beyond yourself. You will find a reward beyond your wildest imagination if your love follows this noble path.

Don't ever forget kindness and truth.
Wear them like a necklace. Write
them on your heart as if on a tablet.

Proverbs 3:3 NCV

Forever

True love weathers every storm and outlasts every trouble. Make your love the kind of love that shelters you forever. Build a relationship with your beloved that will comfort you in your old age.

She is as lovely and graceful as a deer.
Let her love always make you happy;
let her love always hold you captive.

Proverbs 5:19 NCV

Finances

*A*rguments about money can dim the pleasures you deserve to have with your beloved. Discuss with your mate how you both think your money should be spent. If you can both agree on a budget, your life together will be more mutually satisfying.

Houses and wealth are inherited
from parents, but a wise wife
is a gift from the LORD.

Proverbs 19:14 NCV

Loving Sex

*L*oving sex binds a marriage together. Love your spouse unconditionally. Without reserve. Don't use sex as a reward for good behavior or as a threat to get what you want. Love each other abundantly and well.

The wife does not have full rights over her own body; her husband shares them. And the husband does not have full rights over his own body; his wife shares them.

1 Corinthians 7:4 NCV

One Mind

*S*eek harmony in your relationship with your loved one. Don't take detours to total agreement. Talk about your differences until there is full understanding. Do not be afraid of a healthy compromise. Live with your beloved in peace.

Finally, brethren, farewell. Become complete. Be of good comfort, be of one mind, live in peace; and the God of love and peace will be with you.

2 Corinthians 13:11

Judgment

ood judgment helps pave the way to a lasting and whole relationship with the one you love. Seek wisdom as you live your lives together. If you lack wisdom, ask of God and He will supply your need.

And this I pray, that your love may abound still more and more in knowledge and all discernment.

Philippians 1:9

Savor

*L*ove has a sweet savor. Enjoy the essence of the love you share. Be extravagant often, and give yourselves perfumes and ointments that delight the senses. Rejoice in the love of your hearts.

Ointment and perfume
delight the heart.

Proverbs 27:9

Lovemaking

*M*ake love to your spouse with abandon. God has given you marriage for pleasure as well as for family ties. Enjoy your nights together as much as you cherish your days.

Marriage should be honored by
everyone, and husband and wife
should keep their marriage pure.
God will judge as guilty those
who take part in sexual sins.

Hebrews 13:4 NCV

Actions

*P*ut actions behind your sweet words of love. Don't just say, "I love you." Show your beloved how much you care. Look for things you can do to please your mate— *every day.*

My little children, let us not
love in word or in tongue,
but in deed and in truth.

1 John 3:18

Temptation

o not yield to the temptation to take another into your arms. Adultery may seem a pleasant diversion, but the end result can be the death of a marriage. Be true to the one you love, and relish in your mate's uniqueness and beauty.

But each one is tempted when
he is drawn away by his own
desires and enticed. Then, when
desire has conceived, it gives
birth to sin; and sin, when it is
full-grown, brings forth death.

James 1:14–15

Bonded

God is the One who joined you together with your beloved. He is the one who ordained marriage between a man and a woman. If you need guidance in your marriage—and you will—ask for it from the One who abundantly and freely gives.

"And God said, 'So a man will leave his father and mother and be united with his wife, and the two will become one body.' So there are not two, but one. God has joined the two together, so no one should separate them."

Matthew 19:5–6 ncv

Patience

Be patient in your love. Don't insist on returning a harsh word that has been spoken. Don't always try to make the last parting shot in an argument. Love your spouse even when your mate is not acting in love.

"For if you love those who love you,
what reward have you? Do not even
the tax collectors do the same?"

Matthew 5:46

Uplift

*I*f you feel you need strength to continue to love your mate, don't despair. God has promised to give His all-encompassing strength to those who ask it of Him. So be patient and prayerfully wait.

Wait on the LORD;
be of good courage,
and He shall strengthen your heart;
wait, I say, on the LORD!

Psalm 27:14

Patterns

Develop godlike patterns in your life with your beloved. Ask yourself how God would like you to treat your mate. Never settle for less. Be kind; be patient; be filled with loving mercy.

"Therefore be merciful, just as your Father also is merciful."

Luke 6:36

Conversation

A spouse's conversation can be like the sound of constant dripping water—nagging and irritating. Or it can gladden the heart like a bubbling stream. Let your words be ever pleasant.

In the same way, you wives should yield to your husbands. Then, if some husbands do not obey God's teaching, they will be persuaded to believe without anyone's saying a word to them. They will be persuaded by the way their wives live.

1 Peter 3:1 ncv

Growing
Together

Goodness

od crowns each year of our life with His goodness. His mercy and love cushion us from life's hard blows. His care goes before us, and He prepares a way for us through all our days.

You crown the year with Your
goodness, and Your paths
drip with abundance.

Psalm 65:11

Fruitfulness

As a new day begins, remember that God has brought you and your loved one together for a life of joy and fruitfulness. Don't settle for less.

They shall still bear fruit in old age;
they shall be fresh and flourishing.

Psalm 92:14

Families

hank God for your friends and family. The bonds of love that draw you to each other are blessed by God. He wants you to rejoice in the ties of love He has given you.

God gives the lonely a home.
He leads prisoners out with joy,
but those who turn against
God will live in a dry land.

Psalm 68:6 NCV

Prayer

*P*rayer cements your heart to the heart of your beloved. Take time to pray with the special one you love. In praying, you draw near to the soul of the one who means so much to you.

"For where two or three are
gathered together in My name, I
am there in the midst of them."

Matthew 18:20

Family Resources Center
415 NE Monroe,
Peoria, IL 61603 (309) 839-2287

Choices

*L*ove has its price. When you stand with your beloved, you cannot always stand with the rest of the world. But it is the willingness to make this choice that is a sign of true love.

So a man will leave his father and mother and be united with his wife, and the two will become one body.

Genesis 2:24 NCV

Joyful

Embrace your beloved with a joyful heart. Be happy and delight in the smile, the kiss, and the love of the one who fills your heart. Let your joy shine in your eyes and be evident in the words of your mouth.

Let the field be joyful,
and all that is in it.
Then all the trees of the woods
will rejoice before the LORD.

Psalm 96:12

A Seed

Your love grows from a seed that God planted in your heart. No one succeeds in truly loving another unless God gives him or her the ability. It's God who makes your love flourish. Remember Him in worship and prayer.

Those who are planted in the
house of the LORD shall flourish
in the courts of our God.

Psalm 92:13

Warmth

Lying in bed with your loved one keeps you warm through all of life's seasons. When you are together in your intimacy, you can forget the storms that rage outside. So draw near to each other and be warm.

Again, if two lie down together,
they will keep warm; but how
can one be warm alone?

Ecclesiastes 4:11

Seek

You and your beloved both grow as you seek to know God better. Don't be content with a glimpse of Him. Search the Scriptures and yearn to see His face clearly. He'll show Himself to those who seek Him.

Depend on the LORD and his strength; always go to him for help.

Psalm 105:4 NCV

Peace

God promises you peace as you draw near to Him. When you are bitter or angry, don't keep your feelings to yourself. Talk about them with a friend. Then bring your concerns to a God who loves you. He will give you peace.

Great peace have those who
love Your law, and nothing
causes them to stumble.

Psalm 119:165

Sharing

Share your troubles with your beloved. Together you can work to turn your troubles into triumphs. No one is able to do alone what two can do together, especially when it comes to prayer.

Now Isaac pleaded with the LORD
for his wife, because she was barren;
and the LORD granted his plea, and
Rebekah his wife conceived.

Genesis 25:21

Scripture

*D*on't neglect the reading of God's Word with your beloved. Spending time together getting to know God better is one of the richest joys you will know as a couple. His Word will delight and strengthen you.

Your word is very pure;
therefore Your servant loves it.

Psalm 119:140

Beloved

*G*od blesses the pleasure you share with the one you have married. Savor the sweetness of sleeping in your beloved's arms. Carry the sweetness into the day; let it be a comfort to you.

A bundle of myrrh is my
beloved to me, that lies all
night between my breasts.

Song of Solomon 1:13

One

One of the joys and mysteries of life is the way in which a man and woman can become one. The two come together physically, emotionally, and spiritually. They are no longer two; they are one.

"And the two shall become
one flesh; so then they are no
longer two, but one flesh."

Mark 10:8

Disagreements

ncontrollable anger can destroy love. Learn to make your anger a tool to resolve problems rather than let it become a problem in and of itself. Don't let anger build inside until you explode. Handle each day's disagreements within the day itself.

He who is slow to anger is better
than the mighty, and he who rules
his spirit than he who takes a city.

Proverbs 16:32

Power

*P*ower and love—how do they mix? Each couple needs to pray and consider how they are to relate to one another. Without love, power is harsh. When there is love, there is no need for power.

But I want you to understand this:
The head of every man is Christ,
the head of a woman is the man,
and the head of Christ is God.

1 Corinthians 11:3 NCV

Joined

God made wedding vows as strong as steel and as fragile as cut glass. Protect and honor the promises you've made to your beloved. Don't let anyone come between you and your spouse.

"God has joined the two together,
so no one should separate them."

Mark 10:9 NCV

Cleave

*L*earn to hold your loved one tightly. Don't take the one you love for granted. Tell your beloved of your feelings. Love is a precious gift and needs to be cherished. Say, "I love you," today.

"For this reason a man shall leave his father and mother and be joined to his wife."

Mark 10:7

Critics

When others criticize your beloved, don't join in. Be supportive of your mate. Temper any of your own criticisms with the solid assurance that you are on your lover's side.

An enemy might defeat one person,
but two people together can defend
themselves; a rope that is woven
of three strings is hard to break.

Ecclesiastes 4:12 NCV

Satisfied

s you grow to know your beloved, grow also to know the Lord who watches over both of you. Spend time meditating on the Word of God. Do not be content with only a surface knowledge of the Savior. Dig deeply into the riches of His presence.

As for me, I will see Your face in righteousness; I shall be satisfied when I awake in Your likeness.

Psalm 17:15

Renewal

*I*f you have made a major mistake in your relationship with your beloved, don't despair. Be thankful that it's always possible to begin anew. Ask your mate for forgiveness and a clean slate. With God's help, you can and will enjoy an even more fruitful and satisfying life together.

Create in me a clean heart, O God,
and renew a steadfast spirit within me.

Psalm 51:10

Honesty

Speak honestly to your mate. Don't be politely silent when hurt and anger pulse through your veins. Honest words spoken in love make your relationship grow and flourish.

The words of his mouth were smoother than butter, but war was in his heart; his words were softer than oil, yet they were drawn swords.

Psalm 55:21

Each Other

*T*ake time to enjoy your beloved. Refresh your spirit and your love with time together in a quiet, special place. Forget your troubles for a moment, and speak only of the love you share.

Like an apple tree among the trees
of the woods, so is my beloved
among the sons. I sat down in his
shade with great delight, and his
fruit was sweet to my taste.

Song of Solomon 2:3

Mercy

Don't try to hold your marriage together by yourself. Ask God for His grace and mercy on your union. God specializes in healing broken hearts. He brings His oil of love and kindness to households where peace is in short supply.

But I am like a green olive tree in
the house of God; I trust in the
mercy of God forever and ever.

Psalm 52:8

One Flesh

*L*ove draws you close to your beloved until the lines that separate you grow indistinct. God's Word says that marriage vows bring people together until they are flesh of the same flesh and bone of the same bone.

And Adam said: "This is now bone
of my bones and flesh of my flesh;
she shall be called Woman, because
she was taken out of Man."

Genesis 2:23

Hands Filled

Riches do not bring happiness. Finding peace with your beloved will. Expensive presents will never make up for unloving actions. Learn to love with your actions and not with your wallet or purse alone.

Better a handful with quietness
than both hands full, together with
toil and grasping for the wind.

Ecclesiastes 4:6

Distance

ove's first breath can be sweet. But true love grows with the years until the first part of love is only a shadow of the real tie that binds a couple together after a lifetime of love.

The end of a thing is better than
its beginning; the patient in spirit
is better than the proud in spirit.

Ecclesiastes 7:8

Comforting
Each Other

Together

You don't need to bear your troubles all alone. Speak openly to your beloved about the deepest concerns of your heart. Then together go to God in prayer, asking Him to lift your burden and ease your anxiety. Let a gracious and loving Savior help you with your every challenge.

Cast your burden on the Lord,
and He shall sustain you;
He shall never permit the
righteous to be moved.

Psalm 55:22

Mourning

*H*old your mate tightly when trouble enters your relationship and begins to shake your lives. Don't be afraid to cry and to feel your feelings to their very edges. God made you *and* your emotions and put them into one body called YOU! Tears cleanse. Frustration, when dealt with in love, can bring about healing. God also wants you to tell Him how you feel so He can provide for you the comfort He promises.

"Blessed are those who mourn,
for they shall be comforted."

Matthew 5:4

Encouragement

Don't comfort your beloved from a standpoint of weakness. Be strong. Have courage. Speak the truth in love. Comfort your spouse in a way that brings encouragement. Help build on strengths that already exist. Remember that life has many seasons and that troubles come and go. You always have reason to hope.

So encourage each other and
give each other strength, just
as you are doing now.

1 Thessalonians 5:11 NCV

Refuge

*G*od doesn't ask you to have blind trust in Him. He knows your troubles and that their pain often overwhelms you. That's why He offers you and your beloved a refuge, an ever-present haven during the stormy times. Come to Him together in prayer, and let Him give you the delight of His own heart.

Trust in Him at all times, you people;
pour out your heart before Him;
God is a refuge for us.

Psalm 62:8

Not Impossible

Don't give up hope when the dreams you have for you and your beloved appear impossible. God specializes in making the impossible possible. He enjoys helping you make your dreams come true. Talk to Him about what is on your heart. Do it now.

But Jesus looked at them and said, "With men it is impossible, but not with God; for with God all things are possible."

Mark 10:27

Submission

When you find it difficult to be patient because of conflicts you're experiencing with your mate, remember that God has asked you to maintain your love relationship in spite of these challenges. Be patient and help ease the troubles of the one you love. Read 1 Corinthians 13 to help you put your relationship back on course.

❧

Wives, submit to your own husbands,
as to the Lord. . . . Husbands, love
your wives, just as Christ also loved
the church and gave Himself for her.

Ephesians 5:22, 25

Cheer

Comfort your beloved with words of understanding and cheer. Don't be one to focus your conversation on your troubles. God loves a cheerful heart . . . and so will the one with whom you live.

Worry is a heavy load,
but a kind word cheers you up.

Proverbs 12:25 NCV

The Past

When you are feeling sad, take a few moments to remember how God has worked in the life of you and your beloved in the past. Take comfort from the past successes you have enjoyed together.

I remembered Your judgments of old,
O LORD, and have comforted myself.

Psalm 119:52

Healing

You never need to fix the pieces of a broken heart alone. Take sadness to friends and especially to that Friend who sticks closer than a brother, Jesus Christ. He promises to heal the wounds of those who call Him Lord.

The LORD is near to those who
have a broken heart, and saves
such as have a contrite spirit.

Psalm 34:18

Inadequate

When you feel inadequate because you feel you cannot ease the pain of your beloved, remember that God is the One who brings about the healing of body and spirit. Bring your beloved to Him in earnest prayer. God is faithful and promises to listen to your most desperate plea.

A woman whose daughter had an evil spirit in her heard that he was there. So she quickly came to Jesus and fell at his feet. . . . The woman went home and found her daughter lying in bed; the demon was gone.

Mark 7:25, 30 NCV

Gladness

Every marriage has its own special ups and downs. No man or woman has ever been perfect in his or her love. As you recognize your own humanity, ask God to take the hurts in your relationship and show you and your beloved how to turn your greatest challenges into triumphs.

You have turned for me my
mourning into dancing;
You have put off my sackcloth
and clothed me with gladness.

Psalm 30:11

Morning

*H*old your spouse closely when you face grief together. Weep together over your losses. But remember that God is able to turn your night of darkness into a wonderful, ful-filling morning of light and joy.

For His anger is but for a moment,
His favor is for life; weeping
may endure for a night, but
joy comes in the morning.

Psalm 30:5

Death

The death of a loving parent can shake you and your beloved to your core. It may be extremely difficult to accept this great loss. However, as you and your spouse grieve together, be thankful to a merciful God that He has given someone to share your deepest pain.

Then Isaac brought Rebekah into
the tent of Sarah, his mother, and
she became his wife. Isaac loved
her very much, and so he was
comforted after his mother's death.

Genesis 24:67 NCV

Hiding

Sometimes the heartaches in your life will seem like they are simply too much to bear. But never forget that you and your mate have a special hiding place. The Word of God promises you that your heavenly Father comforts and hides His children under His wings.

Keep me as the apple of Your eye;
hide me under the shadow
of Your wings.

Psalm 17:8

Rest

God never suggested He would take away all your burdens in life. You and your beloved will both struggle until the day you die. That is simply the formula known as life! But God has promised to make your burdens lighter, never to give you more than you can bear, and to give you His divine rest as you carry them.

"Come to Me, all you who
labor and are heavy laden,
and I will give you rest."

Matthew 11:28

Bravery

ometimes you will have to do things that may frighten you. Perhaps you'll need to change jobs, move to a new city, or move out of your "comfort zone" to take on a brand-new challenge. Be brave and live today and always in the awareness that you can be confident that God goes before you and will give you the strength you need.

Be of good courage,
and He shall strengthen your heart,
all you who hope in the LORD.

Psalm 31:24

Maturity

As you and your beloved grow to maturity, you will see that it was during the really *tough times* that you developed your stability, resolve, and inner strength. Be comforted in your troubles because that is one way in which an all-knowing God shapes and perfects you.

We do not enjoy being disciplined.
It is painful at the time, but later,
after we have learned from it,
we have peace, because we
start living in the right way.

Hebrews 12:11 NCV

Fair Treatment

Don't count on seeing God's fair treatment only in heaven. The psalmist says that God works justice in our earthly lives as well. In the *here and now*! Ask a just and loving God to work in your life and to keep you faithful to Him at all times. Whatever the cost.

I truly believe I will live to see
the Lord's goodness.

Psalm 27:13 NCV

Home

In the stress and challenges of life, sometimes you may forget that your physical presence is a comfort to your mate. Make it a point to be with your beloved in person when you know your loved one is going through difficult times.

A man who has just married must not be sent to war or be given any other duty. He should be free to stay home for a year to make his new wife happy.

Deuteronomy 24:5 NCV

Alteration

t's a law of nature—your life is going to be filled with alterations both good and bad. God is able to work in every circumstance of your life. Sadness may be for a night, but joy, fulfillment, and comfort will visit you in the morning.

There is a time to throw away stones
and a time to gather them. There
is a time to hug and a time not to
hug. There is a time to look for
something and a time to stop looking
for it. There is a time to keep things
and a time to throw things away.

Ecclesiastes 3:5–6 NCV

Watchful

At times you may wonder if God is either sleeping or dead. Well, don't despair. The psalmist reminds us that God never sleeps nor slumbers. He is always awake, attentive, and aware of the trials that face you. Start trusting Him in a new way. Start this adventure today!

He will not allow your foot
to be moved; He who keeps
you will not slumber.

Psalm 121:3

Needs

*D*on't engage in excessive worry about your daily needs. God watches over all His creation, and He sees and knows what is vital for your sustenance. Come to Him with your beloved, and tell Him of the things you need each day. Come to Him in love and faith—believing He will do what He promises.

"God clothes the grass in the field, which is alive today but tomorrow is thrown into the fire. So you can be even more sure that God will clothe you. Don't have so little faith!"

Matthew 6:30 NCV

Closer

Sometimes it may feel like God is very far away from you and the ones you hold dear. But in reality, God is near at hand no matter where you are—from the top of the highest mountain to the bottom of the deepest ocean. Remember His promise: *I will never leave you nor forsake you*. Live in that awareness of His closeness to you.

If I take the wings of the morning,
and dwell in the uttermost parts of the sea,
even there Your hand shall lead me,
and Your right hand shall hold me.

Psalm 139:9–10

Tears

When you are unhappy, imagine yourself being held tightly in the arms of God your Father. Sometimes you must travel deep into the valley of tears before you can begin to scale the great mountain of joy. Remember, unhappiness does not last forever.

Those who sow in tears
shall reap in joy.

Psalm 126:5

Redeem

New life arises out of sorrow. As you comfort yourself and your beloved, think about how you can redeem your hard times. Learn to bring good out of what, for the moment, seems bad. Adapt your thinking to that of the apostle Paul . . . and be content in whatever circumstances you and your spouse find yourselves.

Then David comforted Bathsheba
his wife, and went in to her and lay
with her. So she bore a son, and
he called his name Solomon.

2 Samuel 12:24

Why?

Throughout history, people have asked God, "Why, Lord, why?" You are not alone if you feel yourself asking this question day after day. Be bold and free enough to ask God to give you understanding of His deepest mysteries.

I want them to be strengthened and
joined together with love so that they
may be rich in their understanding.
This leads to their knowing fully
God's secret, that is, Christ himself.

Colossians 2:2 ncv

Agreement

*L*oneliness can weigh heavily on you when you face a difficult decision. If you and your mate cannot agree on the path you are about to take, agree to disagree without pulling away from each other.

Insults have broken my heart
and left me weak. I looked for
sympathy, but there was none; I
found no one to comfort me.

Psalm 69:20 NCV

Presence

Be fierce in your loyalty to your mate. Don't let others belittle the one you love. Show your beloved that you can be counted on no matter what situations arise.

So Jonathan arose from the table in fierce anger, and ate no food the second day of the month, for he was grieved for David, because his father had treated him shamefully.

1 Samuel 20:34

Safety

God promises you and your beloved a safe dwelling place in Him. Bring your hurts and disappointments to your loving Father, who wants only His best for you. Don't try to face life all on your own. Live your life by living and loving together.

But whoever listens to me
will dwell safely, and will be
secure, without fear of evil.

Proverbs 1:33

Discouragement

G rief and loss come to all of us. You and your spouse are no exception. When you sense that your life is empty and you are discouraged, talk with God—and with your mate—about how you feel, and discuss ways in which you can rise above the circumstances and meet life head-on with joy and enthusiasm.

I am weary with my crying;
my throat is dry; my eyes fail
while I wait for my God.

Psalm 69:3

Refreshment

Say, "I love you," often to your spouse. Many hearts have grown dry waiting to hear those three precious words. Say them often with deep feeling, and they will make your relationship a refreshing oasis in the desert.

Repent therefore and be converted,
that your sins may be blotted out, so
that times of refreshing may come
from the presence of the Lord.

Acts 3:19

Accepting
One Another

Captivate

*L*ove captivates the beloved and holds with soft bonds of affection. Thoughts of personal desires and freedom pale beside the promise of plunging to the depths of another's heart and spirit. This is what true, self-giving love is all about.

I am my beloved's, and my beloved is mine. He feeds his flock among the lilies.

Song of Solomon 6:3

Peace

Resentment and unresolved anger slice through love. They inflict wounds that may take a lifetime of recovery. Give up those grudges that may one day turn to cold anger. Tell your beloved how you feel, and seek to live together in peace.

The LORD will give strength to
His people; the LORD will bless
His people with peace.

Psalm 29:11

Privacy

*T*rust is built when two people keep and cherish each other's secrets. Protect your beloved's privacy with the same care you use to guard your own. Show your faithfulness to your mate in this manner.

Gossips can't keep secrets,
but a trustworthy person can.

Proverbs 11:13 NCV

Wrongs

True love doesn't keep score of the wrongs of another. If you continue to tally the wrongs of your beloved and refuse to let go of the past, you simply cannot grow into a relationship filled with grace and forgiveness. Forgive and forget. You will both be the winners in the long run.

If You, LORD, should mark iniquities,
O Lord, who could stand?
But *there is* forgiveness with You,
that You may be feared.

Psalm 130:3–4

Change

True love must stretch like rubber when personal growth begins to take place. Give your beloved room to be God's whole, complete person. Be an encouragement, not a discouragement. Recognize that *change* is an important part of development.

I may give away everything I have,
and I may even give my body as an
offering to be burned. But I gain
nothing if I do not have love.

1 Corinthians 13:3 NCV

Justice

God is the judge of your actions. He will either reward or discipline you for your deeds. Don't waste time acting as judge, jury, and executioner of your beloved's actions. God will deliver His own appropriate justice to all people. Your task is to love, listen, and care for the one you love.

❧

But God is the Judge: He puts down one, and exalts another.

Psalm 75:7

Approval

*T*ruth is a precious gift given freely to you and your beloved. It's simply yours for the taking. Telling the truth is the key to being known by each other and feeling the wondrous release of being wholly approved of by your beloved. With true approval lies great peace.

Love takes no pleasure in evil
but rejoices over the truth.

1 Corinthians 13:6 NCV

Value

Your words of love are of more value than the costliest pearls. Give your love words freely to your beloved. Don't let a lack of self-confidence or doubt rob you and your beloved of the joy of sharing expressions that speak of romance and affection.

Even a fool is counted wise when he holds his peace; when he shuts his lips, he is considered perceptive.

Proverbs 17:28

Kindness

Kindness must be woven through the fabric of the love you hold for your beloved. This thread must be strong enough to hold the more fragile emotions together. Seek to be kind to your mate. Look for special ways to be gentle and sensitive. Together you can weather any storm.

And be kind to one another,
tenderhearted, forgiving one another,
even as God in Christ forgave you.

Ephesians 4:32

Anger

Unresolved anger opens wounds and causes pain to spread throughout the relationship with your spouse. Cleanse your wounds before anger can take over. Be honest with your feelings. Anger is based on hurt, fear, or frustration. Deal with the real issues—in truth and love.

It is better to live alone in the desert
than with a quarreling and
complaining wife.

Proverbs 21:19 NCV

Thoughts

Fill your mind with wondrous thoughts of the good things God has given you and your beloved—the life you share, the love that draws you to each other, the faith that helps you grow.

Finally, brethren, whatever things
are true, whatever things are noble,
whatever things are just, whatever
things are pure, whatever things are
lovely, whatever things are of good
report, if there is any virtue and if
there is anything praiseworthy—
meditate on these things.

Philippians 4:8

Understanding

Love can easily be clouded over with discouragement and despair. Sometimes you will find yourself confused, not knowing which direction to turn for help in your relationship. The good news is that God promises to give you His understanding in all matters. Lean on Him for His mercy and guidance.

But if any of you needs wisdom,
you should ask God for it. He is
generous to everyone and will give
you wisdom without criticizing you.

James 1:5 NCV

Esteem

*L*ove is a dance of poetry. Each lover bows to the other and says, "No, please, you go first." Bring the poetry of *"you first"* into your relationship with your beloved. Outdo each other, showing love for the other. It will sweeten your love and make it stronger.

When you do things, do not let selfishness or pride be your guide. Instead, be humble and give more honor to others than to yourselves.

Philippians 2:3 ncv

Defenseless

*Y*ou and your beloved stand naked before your Father in heaven, stripped of your defenses, apologies, and excuses. He sees—and miraculously loves—the real, untarnished *you*! Give thanks for His acceptance.

And above all things have fervent love for one another, for "love will cover a multitude of sins."

1 Peter 4:8

Heart

God has a cozy place for you and your spouse in His Fatherly heart. When you are sad, He invites you to come to Him and share your every burden. He will share His heart with you and give you peace. Come into His heart today and feel His love.

And we have known and believed
the love that God has for us. God
is love, and he who abides in love
abides in God, and God in him.

1 John 4:16

Rekindle

Remember the first recognition of mutual love you shared with your beloved—the excitement, the rush of ecstasy, the tingle of fear? Rekindle the passion of those first moments of love. Treat your spouse kindly today, as you did on your first date. You may be amazed at the response.

Nevertheless I have this against you,
that you have left your first love.

Revelation 2:4

Contagious

Love is wonderfully contagious. God's loving-kindness to you can prompt you to acts of loving-kindness to your spouse. Let your whole household be infected with the joy of loving. Spread that joy today—wherever you are and in whatever you do.

Dear friends, if God loved us that much we also should love each other.

1 John 4:11 NCV

Unseen

he path of love often leads through webs of pain and hope often unobserved by others. Your private fears and dreams are yours alone until you share them with that special one you love. Explore unseen places gently.

That path no bird knows,
nor has the falcon's eye seen it.

Job 28:7

Forgiving

rue love has weak eyesight. Faults are not seen and imperfections not noted. So open your life wide to the forgiving eyes of your beloved. Only in openness is knowing one another possible.

"For every tree is known by its own fruit. For men do not gather figs from thorns, nor do they gather grapes from a bramble bush."

Luke 6:44

Innermost

Ask God to spread His light of love around the hearts of you and your beloved. His light will be the laser beam of Truth that helps you know each other in your innermost being. Delve deeply to the core of your togetherness. Such knowing is the foundation of love.

God's lamp shined on my head, and I walked through darkness by his light.

Job 29:3 NCV

Benefits

Woo your beloved with affectionate words and pleasing ways. Drink your mate's refreshing nectar. Seek to know your spouse more deeply with every day you share together. Recognize the value of your every moment together. A relationship filled with love makes you a wealthy couple indeed.

Praise the LORD, God our Savior,
who helps us every day.

Psalm 68:19 NCV

Perfection

*G*od has provided marriage as one way for His children to grow to perfection. When someone knows you as well as your spouse, you can always run . . . *but you can never hide!* Use your learning about one another to encourage growth.

Therefore, beloved, looking
forward to these things, be diligent
to be found by Him in peace,
without spot and blameless.

2 Peter 3:14

Fight

*T*roubles can steal the seeds of your marital happiness before you can plant them. Fight the troubles. Store the seeds well. Together with your mate, ask God to help you overcome all your difficulties. He is faithful to grant you His counsel and wisdom. Take advantage of it.

The LORD your God will go ahead
of you and fight for you as he did
in Egypt; you saw him do it.

Deuteronomy 1:30 NCV

Enticement

*L*ove is a powerful persuader and seducer. Use your love to draw your mate closer to the heart of the One True God. Guard your own faith so your mate does not entice you away from Him.

Someone might try to lead
you to serve other gods. . . . Do
not give in to such people.

Deuteronomy 13:6, 8 NCV

Foundation

Build your marriage upon the sure foundation of a shared faith and hope in the Lord Jesus Christ. If you and your beloved are aiming at the same targets, your opportunities for growth and fulfillment are magnified many times over.

"Everyone who hears my words
and obeys them is like a wise man
who built his house on rock."

Matthew 7:24 NCV

Longings

When you lie in your bed at night, loneliness may sometimes flood your soul even though your mate is lying by your side. See this as your inner yearning for the God who promises to fill your innermost being with joy.

My soul breaks with longing
for Your judgments at all times.

Psalm 119:20

Planting

Sow seeds of righteousness and joy in your relationship with your beloved mate. Cultivate happiness together. God will cause the seeds to grow to full bloom when you make Him first in your lives.

The earth causes plants to grow, and
a garden causes the seeds planted
in it to grow. In the same way the
Lord GOD will make goodness and
praise come from all the nations.

Isaiah 61:11 NCV

Nature

*E*njoy all of the pleasures of the senses with your beloved. Walk together on a balmy afternoon. Enjoy a stroll in the gentle rain. Put the cares of business aside, and make a date with your spouse today. After all, your beloved *is* the most important person in your life.

The flowers appear on the earth;
the time of singing has come,
and the voice of the turtledove
is heard in our land.

Song of Solomon 2:12

Talent

Strive to look at yourself clearly. God has given you a multitude of gifts and talents. He has given perhaps similar—or perhaps much different—talents to your mate. Encourage yourself and your spouse to develop all the talents God has given you both. Do the very best with the equipment you have. It's all you'll ever need.

"And to one he gave five talents, to another two, and to another one, to each according to his own ability; and immediately he went on a journey."

Matthew 25:15

Being
Companions

Concentrate

*L*ove has many dimensions and can make you more scattered or more centered. Concentrate and seek to be of one mind with your mate. Discuss what you both want for your relationship, and then pull together to reach that goal.

Finally, all of you should be in agreement, understanding each other, loving each other as family, being kind and humble.

1 Peter 3:8 NCV

Movement

Your love relationship orbits around God even as the moon moves around the earth. God keeps your relationship moving, fluid and dynamic. Always remember that your heavenly Father is the One behind all the love you give and receive.

For You, O God, have tested us;
You have refined us as silver is refined.

Psalm 66:10

Rejoice

*F*avor the companionship you share with your beloved. Breathe deeply of the beautiful fragrance of your love. Rejoice in the blessings you enjoy as a couple.

Let your fountain be blessed,
and rejoice with the wife of your youth.

Proverbs 5:18

Increase

The first taste of love can strike you like a thunderbolt. But it's the steady, constant companionship and friendship that makes that first moments of passion grow into a love to endure for a lifetime. Grow with your beloved.

May the Lord make your love grow
more and multiply for each other
and for all people so that you will
love others as we love you.

1 Thessalonians 3:12 NCV

Intertwined

You and your beloved are intertwined. The love you have for each other shines all around you—and the world smiles at your devotion. Keep your love shining. Never betray the love you share with your mate.

An excellent wife is the crown of her husband, but she who causes shame is like rottenness in his bones.

Proverbs 12:4

Salvation

Deep in the soul of every man and woman is the desire to know God and experience His divine love. Honor that desire in your mate, and make God the cornerstone of your marriage.

Let all those who seek You rejoice
and be glad in You; and let those
who love Your salvation say
continually, "Let God be magnified!"

Psalm 70:4

Romance

*L*ive in the heart of your beloved. Risk romance with the one you love. Speak the poetry of your love even if the words don't seem like polished gems to you. Your lover will treasure the words.

Then she said, "Let me find favor
in your sight, my lord; for you have
comforted me, and have spoken kindly
to your maidservant, though I am
not like one of your maidservants."

Ruth 2:13

Distinguish

God sees the hidden heart of everyone. Give your innermost thoughts to God in prayer. Let Him help you and your mate distinguish and separate the good from the bad that you might be more fruitful for Him.

The LORD looks down from
heaven upon the children of
men, to see if there are any who
understand, who seek God.

Psalm 14:2

Cry Out

Cry out to God when you feel lonely. Loneliness can engulf you and leave you floating on an endless sea of despair. Ask God to bring you comfort, and trust Him to help you.

Loved one and friend You
have put far from me, and my
acquaintances into darkness.

Psalm 88:18

Friendship

*L*ove has many faces. Its most beautiful countenance is the face of friendship. Cultivate a deep, lasting friendship with your beloved. Play together with abandon, share your interests, take long walks, and learn to be one heart in two bodies.

A friend loves at all times, and a brother is born for adversity.

Proverbs 17:17

Righteous

When you love, your soul meets and kisses the good that is inside the soul of your beloved. Nurture that which is righteous, correct, and noble in your beloved, and let your beloved encourage those same qualities within you.

Mercy and truth have met together;
righteousness and peace have kissed.

Psalm 85:10

Confidential

CONFIDENTIAL should be stamped across your love relationship in large red letters. The privacy you give your beloved makes it possible to tell of your inmost thoughts, feeling secure in the knowledge that they will be safe with your mate.

He who covers a transgression
seeks love, but he who repeats
a matter separates friends.

Proverbs 17:9

Servanthood

True love doesn't worry about who's the boss. It doesn't keep score in the "Whose turn is it now?" game. True love rejoices in doing what is good for your beloved and in serving one another.

"But he who is greatest among you shall be your servant."

Matthew 23:11

Unity

rue love knits two people together until the threads of one life are intertwined with the threads of the other. Celebrate the unity you share with the mate God has given you. Give thanks today—right now—by praising God for what you are sharing together.

Behold, how good and how
pleasant it is for brethren to
dwell together in unity!

Psalm 133:1

Counsel

*A*ny romantic relationship falters at times . . . and only a more mature, wise person can tell you how to rekindle your love. Seek help from others when you do not know how to mend a troubled relationship. Help is near. Be courageous enough to ask for it.

Where there is no counsel, the people fall; but in the multitude of counselors there is safety.

Proverbs 11:14

Essence

Poets have tried for centuries to capture the essence of love. The Bible tells us quite simply that real love is caring more about others than you care for yourself and your own needs. Be a model of selfless love in your relationship. It will be contagious.

But each one of you must love
his wife as he loves himself, and a
wife must respect her husband.

Ephesians 5:33 NCV

Blame

God has given you and your mate different skills and responsibilities. Don't constantly blame your mate for things that are undone. Ask yourself, "Is some of this *my* responsibility?" Work together in harmony and a spirit of companionship.

Better to dwell in a corner of a
housetop, than in a house shared
with a contentious woman.

Proverbs 21:9

Winning

What will you do to show your mate how much your love means? Let your beloved know you'd be willing to go to great lengths if necessary. Then put your actions to work to win your mate all over again. Rekindle your love with a fresh, new commitment.

Now Jacob loved Rachel; so he said,
"I will serve you seven years for
Rachel your younger daughter."

Genesis 29:18

Intellect

When metal strikes metal, both become more finely honed. The same is true with intelligence in two people. Challenge your beloved—and yourself—to greater intellectual thoughts. Read widely; understand broadly; push yourself to greater awareness of the world around you.

As iron sharpens iron,
so a man sharpens the
countenance of his friend.

Proverbs 27:17

Giving Your All

entleness is like oil that smooths the friction of day-to-day living. Gentleness inspires love and affection. Give all that you are, and be extra gentle to your mate as you walk through your days together.

The husband should give his wife
all that he owes her as his wife. And
the wife should give her husband all
that she owes him as her husband.

1 Corinthians 7:3 NCV

Wholeness

*L*ove your mate with your whole body and soul. Luxuriate in the delights of your love. Romance blooms gently in the midst of tenderness and thoughtfulness. Enjoy the love you share.

The whole body depends on Christ, and all the parts of the body are joined and held together. Each part does its own work to make the whole body grow and be strong with love.

Ephesians 4:16 NCV

Like-Minded

ove molds you into many of the shapes and attitudes of your beloved. Seek to grow in positive ways with your mate. Decide together on what is important in the lives you share. You are two . . . but your hearts must beat as one.

If so, make me very happy by
having the same thoughts,
sharing the same love, and
having one mind and purpose.

Philippians 2:2 NCV

Bitterness

Hidden anger and bitterness can turn a love relationship into a cold war. Guard against harbored anger in your heart, and learn to talk to your beloved about any hurts or disappointments that arise.

Wives, yield to the authority of your husbands, because this is the right thing to do in the Lord. Husbands, love your wives and be gentle with them.

Colossians 3:18–19 NCV

Vows

The vows you took on your wedding day are the most life-changing promises you will ever make. Esteem and honor your vows. Never forsake the love that brought you together.

The Scripture says, "So a man will leave his father and mother and be united with his wife, and the two will become one body."

Ephesians 5:31 ncv

Devotion

*G*od's hand is the one that fashioned you and your beloved—your personalities, your intellects, you deepest desires. Rejoice in His presence in your life together, and give Him your devotion.

LORD, You have been our dwelling place in all generations.

Psalm 90:1

Dwelling

God has promised a dwelling place for you. When the difficulties of your life and your relationships seem dry and unfulfilling, come to the Lord who loves you for refreshment and renewed hope.

Firm is your dwelling place,
and your nest is set in the rock.

Numbers 24:21

Arrogance

rrogance can crush love quicker than almost anything. True love is built on acceptance and kindness one toward another. Protect your relationship with your beloved from the harshness of arrogance.

God resists the proud,
but gives grace to the humble.

1 Peter 5:5

Abundance

The very core of love is found in the heart of God. If your love has grown stale, ask God to give you an abundance of the love He so generously gives to those who ask of Him. It's still true—*ask and you shall receive.* Accept His generous offer of love today for you and your beloved.

"By his power we live and move and exist." Some of your own poets have said: "For we are his children."

Acts 17:28 NCV

Listen

A listening heart is a balm to a damaged relationship. Be willing to see your relationship through the eyes of your mate. God has given you ears to hear. Ask Him to help you listen wisely.

The Lord has made both these things:
ears to hear and eyes to see.

Proverbs 20:12 NCV

Working Together

Commitment

The burdens of life may seem to be impossible. Every day you observe your own weaknesses and those of your beloved. Then you remember what brought you together in the first place. You recall that a couple in love can pull a heavier load together than each can pull alone. It's what commitment to "stick together" is all about.

The land has given its crops.

God, our God, blesses us.

Psalm 67:6 NCV

Support

True love is not easily embarrassed. Seek to help work out the plan God has for your beloved's life. Never allow the teasing or ridicule of others to stop you from being 100 percent supportive of your mate. Because when it's all said and done, all you really have on earth is each other.

But Noah found grace in the eyes of the LORD. . . . Then the LORD said to Noah, "Come into the ark, you and all your household, because I have seen that you are righteous before Me in this generation.

Genesis 6:8; 7:1

Aging

An enduring, loving marriage is a wondrous monument to the goodness of a gracious Lord. As your gray hairs begin to appear and as your bodies start to slow down, let your love for each other increase. Your life together is your greatest work for God.

Now also when I am old and
grayheaded, O God, do not forsake
me, until I declare Your strength
to this generation, Your power
to everyone who is to come.

Psalm 71:18

Freedom

hank God daily for the bountiful privileges He has given to you and your spouse. Consider what your marriage and family would be like if you did not have the freedoms you are able to enjoy together. Rejoice in God's blessings. Be thankful for your liberty today.

His descendants will be mighty
on earth; the generation of
the upright will be blessed.

Psalm 112:2

Labor

*L*ove isn't all hugs and laughter. Love that's deep and solid also involves hard work and sweat. Spend time working with your beloved. When it's tough, do it tough. When it's easy, do it easy. Then take the time to stand back and enjoy the fruits of your labor together.

Two *are* better than one,
because they have a good
reward for their labor.

Ecclesiastes 4:9

Benediction

Our Almighty Father, Ruler of the heavens and King of all the earth, wants to bless you today. Gratefully accept His love and kind benediction as you and your beloved go about your daily tasks.

God be merciful to us and bless us,
and cause His face to shine upon us.

Psalm 67:1

Rules

*L*ove does not grow by iron-clad rules that seek to bend others to our own way. Love grows in the gentle breeze of acceptance. Love your mate closer to your heart with gentleness, not legislation.

Love does no harm to a
neighbor; therefore love is
the fulfillment of the law.

Romans 13:10

Weakness

ot all work is done through strength. Some of the best and most enduring work is accomplished when two lovers are at the point of their greatest weakness, both spiritually and physically. Don't wait to be strong to do what God wants you to do. Simply put your hand to the task to be done *today*.

Blessed is the man
whose strength is in You,
whose heart is set on pilgrimage.

Psalm 84:5

The Best

The best part of love is not in its intelligence. Love is notoriously blind. Nor does the best part lie in its unending hope. No, the best part of love is simply in its seeking the very best for your mate—and wanting that "best" for your beloved more than you desire it for yourself.

And though I have the gift of
prophecy, and understand all
mysteries and all knowledge, and
though I have all faith, so that
I could remove mountains, but
have not love, I am nothing.

1 Corinthians 13:2

Workings

Make it a daily decision that you and your mate train your eyes to behold the workings of the Lord. Seek to see His hand in the events around you. Then give outward thanks to Him for His help in the life of your family.

I will also meditate on all Your work, and talk of Your deeds.

Psalm 77:12

Accord

Two hearts don't always beat as one. However, in the most important matters of your life together, seek harmony with your mate so you can experience the joy of life with agreement and a deep sense of meaning and purpose.

"Again I say to you that if two of you agree on earth concerning anything that they ask, it will be done for them by My Father in heaven."

Matthew 18:19

Generations

The desire to mate and build a family is given to people from a God who said, "Be fruitful and multiply on the earth" (Genesis 8:17). It's vital that you and your spouse regard your child-rearing years as among the most fulfilling work of your entire lives. You are designing the world's future.

Your seed I will establish forever,
and build up your throne
to all generations.

Psalm 89:4

Protection

*L*ie down in repose in the warmth of God's love. His power protects you so you can frolic with your beloved. He smiles when He sees the love that flows between you and your mate in your most tender moments.

For the LORD God is a sun and shield;
the LORD will give grace and glory;
no good thing will He withhold
from those who walk uprightly.

Psalm 84:11

Beside

God doesn't stay home in the morning; He goes to work with you. Never forget that He is beside you with each decision and task you need to do during the business day. Ask Him for any wisdom you lack, and He will give it to you from the abundance of a Father's heart.

Is not the LORD your God with you?
And has He not given you rest on
every side? For He has given the
inhabitants of the land into my hand,
and the land is subdued before
the LORD and before His people.

1 Chronicles 22:18

Individuals

God has made you and your mate as individuals. He gave each of you different talents and abilities. Ask Him how He would like you to use these gifts in His service. Always use your gifts to glorify the Lord!

Your hands have made
me and fashioned me;
give me understanding, that I may
learn Your commandments.

Psalm 119:73

Response

ow do you handle criticism? How do you respond to the inadequacies in yourself and others? Are you sensitive to the needs and ambitions of others? Let God teach you to reflect His love and understanding in the workplace.

Always be humble, gentle, and
patient, accepting each other in love.

Ephesians 4:2 NCV

Career

Wisdom from God makes the difference between a successful career and a series of failures. The Bible gives you and your mate a solid foundation for relating justly and honestly to those around you. Ask God for more wisdom to build a strong foundation as you work together to make your relationship a success.

Teach me good judgment
and knowledge, for I believe
Your commandments.

Psalm 119:66

Tapestry

Love is a golden thread that, when woven throughout your days, makes your life a beautiful tapestry for all to see. Don't ration the love you share with your mate. Give your love freely—with an almost reckless abandon. Let your love be a pleasant blend of all that is wonderful and good.

Rest in the LORD, and wait patiently for Him.

Psalm 37:7

Stretch

Make a pact with your spouse to indulge yourselves with the love of God. God specializes in good gifts. The gift of your mate is but one example of God's boundless caring. He has given you a beloved one to love even as He has given Himself generously to you. Stretch your love, and let it grow today.

Every good gift and every perfect gift
is from above, and comes down from
the Father of lights, with whom there
is no variation or shadow of turning.

James 1:17

Ethics

As you and your spouse engage in business, exercise caution in accepting counsel from those whose ethics may be in question. Pick your counselors and business associates with great care. Your reputation, integrity, and honor are at stake.

Blessed is the man who walks not
in the counsel of the ungodly, nor
stands in the path of sinners, nor
sits in the seat of the scornful.

Psalm 1:1

Leadership

God created you and your spouse as natural leaders. In your workplaces, seek ways to demonstrate your leadership skills. Encourage growth in your mate in all areas of life. If you want to be a leader—lead! Others who value your guidance will follow, especially if you have children.

Then God blessed them, and God
said to them, "Be fruitful and multiply;
fill the earth and subdue it; have
dominion over the fish of the sea, over
the birds of the air, and over every
living thing that moves on the earth."

Genesis 1:28

Tithe

*H*onor God with the first place in your affections. Give a worthy portion to Him before you spend liberally on yourself. Agree with your spouse to bring the fruits of your work to God and give them to Him with devotion.

Honor the LORD with your possessions,
and with the firstfruits of all your
increase; so your barns will be
filled with plenty, and your vats
will overflow with new wine.

Proverbs 3:9–10

Occupation

When seeking an occupation, follow your natural abilities and desires. God has given you and your beloved skills unmatched by others. He wants you to use them to His glory. Work diligently as unto the Lord, and He will bless your labor.

Delight yourself also in the LORD,
and He shall give you the
desires of your heart.

Psalm 37:4

Companion

It can be wearisome to feel alone in one's work. A responsive God saw the loneliness in man's heart and made for him a friend, a companion, a wife. Enjoy each other to the fullest. Do something extra special for each other today.

Then the LORD God said, "It is not good for the man to be alone. I will make a helper who is right for him."

Genesis 2:18 NCV

Parenting

Some of the most challenging labor in life takes place in the home. It's difficult to be a parent without having someone else to help you in the hard times. Lean on your spouse for support in raising your children.

If one falls down, the other can help him up. But it is bad for the person who is alone and falls, because no one is there to help.

Ecclesiastes 4:10 NCV

Yardstick

God has set a standard for you and your spouse. Honesty and integrity are among the two most important yardsticks He has created to measure your performance. Is there anything that needs improvement? Talk it over. Listen to each other. If need be, make some changes. Start today.

For the word of the LORD is right,
and all His work is done in truth.

Psalm 33:4

Practical

*L*et God's abundance and love flow through you and your beloved. God generously rewards those who show mercy and kindness to others. Find someone needy to love. Reach out beyond yourselves in practical kindness.

When you reap the harvest of your land, you shall not wholly reap the corners of your field, nor shall you gather the gleanings of your harvest.

Leviticus 19:9

Credit

Always give your beloved verbal credit for a job well done. Know that God rewards His children who honestly and righteously serve Him in the workplace. Encourage yourself and your mate through the difficult times. Be sure to go out of your way to give credit where it's due.

❧

Do you see people skilled in their work? They will work for kings, not for ordinary people.

Proverbs 22:29

Provider

The Lord gives and the Lord takes away. God is the one who controls your destiny and your days. If you or your beloved lack anything, go to the heavenly Father and ask Him. He is pleased to provide for His children.

And He said to them, "Cast the net on the right side of the boat, and you will find some." So they cast, and now they were not able to draw it in because of the multitude of fish.

John 21:6

Being
Known

Known

Your soul cries out to be known by someone special. And even as you are drawn to a deeper, more intimate relationship with your mate, a loving God chooses to draw you both closer to Himself. Your heavenly Father wants to be known, loved, and served. Live in the comfort of knowing that your Father cares.

But as for me, my prayer is to You,
O LORD, in the acceptable time;
O God, in the multitude of Your mercy,
hear me in the truth of Your salvation.

Psalm 69:13

Imperfections

Sing softly of your beloved's virtues. Praise all good things. Let your pride be seen on your face. Let your love for your spouse be a hiding place for your beloved's imperfections.

Even more than all this, clothe
yourself in love. Love is what holds
you all together in perfect unity.

Colossians 3:14 NCV

Hidden

Delight in searching out the hidden places of your beloved's mind and soul. Love the dark, shadowy places, and rejoice where there is light in abundance. Give your heart to your own love and none other. Leave room for hidden mysteries.

Be faithful to your own wife, just as you drink water from your own well.

Proverbs 5:15 NCV

Evening

After the sun has set and darkness covers your face, seek the sweet communion of time spent with your beloved at the merciful throne of your Father. He will give you comfort in the times of trial and sustenance when the challenges seem too great. Believe in His great mercy today.

I call to remembrance my song in
the night; I meditate within my heart,
and my spirit makes diligent search.

Psalm 77:6

Searching

Gaze upon the sleeping face of your beloved. When you were courting, words were not enough to describe your mate's inner and outer beauty. Still, you want to know your beloved in greater depth. Keep the exploration alive today and every day. Never be satisfied. Always know that there is more to be discovered about your beloved.

The spirit of a man is the lamp
of the LORD, searching all the
inner depths of his heart.

Proverbs 20:27

Speech

To some, love comes in a whisper. For others, it arrives with a great, tumultuous shout! But from the beginning, words are important. Words either build or destroy. Let your positive, loving speech—coupled with "love actions"—be the proof of your love.

Let your speech always be with grace,
seasoned with salt, that you may know
how you ought to answer each one.

Colossians 4:6

Criticism

Loving criticism is better than lying praise. The one purifies so wounds can heal. The other breeds infection so that only a temporary peace can be maintained. Speak the truth in love with your mate. Do not shy away from caring, honest reproof.

The slap of a friend can be trusted
to help you, but the kisses of an
enemy are nothing but lies.

Proverbs 27:6 NCV

Politeness

*T*rue politeness is grounded in considerate truth. When seeking to know your beloved, don't be content with anything less than straightforward, honest communication. The roots of true love grow deeply when the truth is spoken with compassion and love.

Keep your tongue from evil, and
your lips from speaking deceit.

Psalm 34:13

Appreciate

Wedding days are rapturous and exciting. Congratulations and happy tears abound. But the wedding day ecstasy cannot endure forever. Each twenty-four hours has its own texture. Appreciate each day for its own value. Like a game of chess, no day is ever the same. Enjoy the difference. Appreciate the variety of your love.

Don't ask, "Why was life
better in the 'good old days'?"
It is not wise to ask such questions.

Ecclesiastes 7:10 NCV

Treasure

*L*ook at the face of your beloved and you will see flashes of gold. In fact, what you see is much more precious than gold. A love rooted and grounded in God makes your lover's countenance shine more brightly than any earthly treasures.

"For where your treasure is,
there your heart will be also."

Luke 12:34

Hate

Hate and love are flip sides of the same coin. And sometimes only a coin's width separates the two. Love can be wounded so severely that it can lose its value and deteriorate into hate and despair. Make both sides of your coin read "I love you." Heads, you win; tails, you win too!

Love suffers long and is kind;
love does not envy; love does not
parade itself, is not puffed up.

1 Corinthians 13:4

Harmony

*L*ove is much like an orchestra responding to the skill and care of a conductor. No single instrument can ever be the sole star. The music and the harmony of all players is what makes it a thing of beauty. Live in that kind of harmony with your spouse. If there is discord in your heart, "conduct it out" today.

Love is patient and kind. Love is
not jealous, it does not brag, and
it is not proud. Love is not rude, is
not selfish, and does not get upset
with others. Love does not count
up wrongs that have been done.

1 Corinthians 13:4–5 NCV

Married

ou married because you "fell in love." Now, as your love matures, you find yourself "standing in love"—an even more mature form of affection. When you truly love, you ask, "What can I do for you?" not, "What are you going to do for me?" Love is an "inside job," but once it emerges, the outward expression of your affection makes a world of difference to your beloved.

In the same way, husbands should
love their wives as they love
their own bodies. The man who
loves his wife loves himself.

Ephesians 5:28 NCV

Pearls

*P*riceless pearls are created in the deep, hidden recesses of the oyster shell. Let your heart and soul be as one of those pearls of great price—quietly growing in value every day. Start living this way today!

It is not fancy hair, gold jewelry, or fine clothes that should make you beautiful. No, your beauty should come from within you— the beauty of a gentle and quiet spirit that will never be destroyed and is very precious to God.

1 Peter 3:3–4 NCV

Flame

Your love can be a quiet, flickering candle or a roaring fire. But your true love has flame *only because God has given you* an *enormous capacity to love*. Thank God for the ability He has freely given to you to share your deepest affection with your beloved.

Beloved, let us love one another, for love is of God; and everyone who loves is born of God and knows God.

1 John 4:7

Stumbling

*L*ove is the light that guides you in your relationship with your beloved. But your love isn't perfect—never has been and never will be. Love can stumble and cause pain. All that is required is for you to put the good of your beloved ahead of your own desires. If you stumble, pick yourself up and start all over again.

***

Whoever loves a brother or sister
lives in the light and will not cause
anyone to stumble in his faith.

1 John 2:10 NCV

Discernment

Not all of the ways of the Lord are plain to our earthly eyes. Sometimes the workings of the Father are subtle and can only be observed by the most discerning mind. Seek to know how God is working in the lives of you and your beloved.

The secret of the Lord is with those who fear Him, and He will show them His covenant.

Psalm 25:14

Pretense

*L*ove makes mistakes. But a willingness to set things right is more important to your beloved than feigned perfection. Don't pretend when you don't know what to do in your relationship. Talk with your beloved. Two-way communication unearths hidden treasure.

People cannot see their own mistakes.
Forgive me for my secret sins.

Psalm 19:12 NCV

Intimacy

When you share from the center of your heart, you give a gift beyond value to your beloved. Take time to give this greatest of all treasures to your spouse. Share your personal secrets with your lover alone. True intimacy will be your reward.

And Adam knew his wife again.

Genesis 4:25

Courage

Courage is the tool that sculpts and refines a loving marriage. It takes courage to tell your beloved that you have been hurt by words or deeds. But do not neglect the cleansing of your hurt feelings. If you do, they will fester and injure your love. Have the courage to speak about your feelings . . . and do it with love in your heart.

—⁂—

"If your fellow believer sins against you, go and tell him in private what he did wrong. If he listens to you, you have helped that person to be your brother or sister again."

Matthew 18:15 NCV

Beauty

Compliments are like a welcome summer breeze after the gales of winter. Tell your beloved of the beauty your eyes see. Speak often of your deep, deep love, and your relationship will blossom. It's still true—you will always reap what you sow. Speak love and you harvest love. Let your marriage be a trophy of caring.

Among the young women, my
darling is like a lily among thorns!

Song of Solomon 2:2 NCV

Bountiful

Our Father in heaven has given you and your beloved a bountiful marriage. Feast on the delights of your love for each other. Rejoice in the sensation of being joined to your beloved. Feel your love to the edges, and live in the exhilaration of your affection.

The man and his wife were naked,
but they were not ashamed.

Genesis 2:25 NCV

Steadfast

The health of your marriage rests on the mercy of a loving, living God. He is the One who can make the rough ways smooth and heal your broken heart. He steadfastly gives strength to you—His child. He is generous, loving, and kind. Rely on His grace to keep your marriage healthy and strong.

It is God who arms me with strength,
and makes my way perfect.

Psalm 18:32

Enchantment

*T*rue love is spun with the purest of golden thoughts. You dream enchanted dreams of the next time you will be alone with your mate. Strangely and beautifully, time both slows down and speeds up when you are in the presence of your beloved. Keep your love alive in fresh, creative ways. Recapture the wonder of your love.

So Jacob served seven years
for Rachel, and they seemed
only a few days to him because
of the love he had for her.

Genesis 29:20

Looking

You look into the face of your beloved, searching for a sign of romantic devotion, for a quickly returned glance of adoration. Then you see it in your beloved's eyes—you are well-loved. You embrace. You have rediscovered why you are standing in love.

After his evening meal, Boaz felt good and went to sleep lying beside the pile of grain. Ruth went to him quietly and lifted the cover from his feet and lay down.

Ruth 3:7 NCV

Hiding Place

Wrap yourself in God's holiness. He wants to be your hiding place when you feel sad and forsaken by those who say they love you. He is waiting to comfort and encourage you every day. He will never leave you nor forsake you. That's His promise to you!

But You, O Lord, are a shield
for me, my glory and the One
who lifts up my head.

Psalm 3:3

Emotions

Your love relationship is a place for you to *know* your emotions, *own* your emotions, and *show* your emotions. Your fears, joys, concerns, hurts, and sky-splitting moments of ecstasy are all part of the person God made you to be. Celebrate them all with your beloved.

From the end of the earth I will
cry to You, when my heart is
overwhelmed; lead me to the
rock that is higher than I.

Psalm 61:2

Promises

Promises broken and promises kept—these two things alternately destroy and build trust. Let the words that come from your mouth be words that come from your heart. Promise your beloved only what you feel you can deliver.

For You, O God, have heard my vows;
You have given me the heritage
of those who fear Your name.

Psalm 61:5

Correction

Comfort is the backbone of love. Accept your beloved for who he or she is. Don't overcorrect your spouse with words of torment or reproof. Learn instead to stand beside your beloved with quiet encouragement. If you need to begin this new behavior, start doing it today.

I have heard many such things;
miserable comforters are you all!

Job 16:2

Living with Hope

Lift Your Eyes

*L*ift your eyes to the Lord of the heavens, and ask Him to shower your love relationship with grace. He is the One who enables you to love. It is He who gives you more ability to love if you ask Him. May His love encompass you and your beloved today.

He shall come down like rain
upon the grass before mowing,
like showers that water the earth.

Psalm 72:6

Kisses

rink your fill of the kisses of your beloved. Savor the warmth of your lover's closeness. God smiles to see the love you share with your mate. Rejoice in your life together.

Kiss me with the kisses of your mouth, because your love is better than wine.

Song of Solomon 1:2 NCV

Shield

W hen enemies are camped around you and your beloved, do not fear. The God who reigns over all the heavens and earth will be your defender and will shield you from harm.

O God, behold our shield,
and look upon the face
of Your anointed.

Psalm 84:9

Capacity

Loving someone is not always easy. Everyone has blocks that often stand in the way. Too many times, old hurts make us cautious in love. Ask God to continue to bring you to maturity and to give you the capacity to love as never before.

God began doing a good work
in you, and I am sure he will
continue it until it is finished when
Jesus Christ comes again.

Philippians 1:6 NCV

Acceptance

*L*ove your mate with confidence. Support your beloved's strengths while not shying away from the weaknesses. They are all part of being human. Believe the best of your mate, even as you accept the frailness of your beloved.

Love patiently accepts all
things. It always trusts, always
hopes, and always endures.

1 Corinthians 13:7 NCV

Merry

ance with your love before the Lord. Be merry in your affection as you serenade each other with laughter. Feel the warm smile of God upon the lives of you and your beloved. Celebrate your togetherness *now*!

Glory in His holy name;
let the hearts of those rejoice
who seek the LORD!

Psalm 105:3

Freely

*G*ive the precious gift of your heart first to God and then to your beloved. Do not hold back. Give of yourself freely without counting the price. You'll be rewarded over and over for your efforts.

While Jesus was there, a woman
approached him with an alabaster
jar filled with expensive perfume.
She poured this perfume on Jesus'
head while he was eating.

Matthew 26:7 NCV

Renewal

*L*ove ebbs and flows. If you are feeling low on affection, ask God to renew the melody of love that once sang in your heart. God is the God of new beginnings. He will give you all that you ask of Him.

You send forth Your Spirit, they
are created; and You renew
the face of the earth.

Psalm 104:30

Gladness

*L*et gladness surround your love and lighten the hearts of all who see the devotion you share with your mate. Treat your beloved like the priceless treasure that God has shaped and designed for you.

He brought out His people with joy,
His chosen ones with gladness.

Psalm 105:43

Persistence

A loving heart binds up hurts with a patient and forgiving spirit. When you or your beloved stumble, don't give up walking toward each other. Everyone makes mistakes in love. Reflect often on what drew you together in the first place. Have patience and rediscover each other as the bond you share strengthens daily.

Now may the Lord direct your
hearts into the love of God and
into the patience of Christ.

2 Thessalonians 3:5

Voice

God spoke the world into being. His voice rang out throughout the universe, and all that lived leaped to obey His command. Ask God to speak into your life with your beloved. Let His love and wisdom be yours in all your dealings this day and always.

The LORD's voice shakes the oaks
and strips the leaves off the trees.
In his Temple everyone
says, "Glory to God!"

Psalm 29:9 NCV

Time

ime belongs to God. Ask Him to make you a wise steward of the twenty-four hours of each day He has given you. Spend time with your spouse, and speak frankly and openly about the concerns of your heart. Always make time for each other.

Then the LORD appointed a set
time, saying, "Tomorrow the LORD
will do this thing in the land."

Exodus 9:5

Learning

Marriage is a great teacher. You see your own faults more clearly when placed up against another's needs. Thank God for His help as you grow into the person He wants you to be. Life is your school, and your mate is one of your best teachers. Learn well today and every day.

God is strong and can help you
not to fall. He can bring you before
his glory without any wrong in
you and can give you great joy.

Jude v. 24 NCV

Oasis

God leads you into pleasant pastures. Ask Him to bring you and your beloved to a quiet oasis where He may give you a time of rest in your life together. Focus on your beloved, and declare all the love that has grown in your heart thus far.

We are your people, the sheep of your flock. We will thank you always; forever and ever we will praise you.

Psalm 79:13 NCV

Blessings

When people receive a great gift, they usually cannot wait to tell everyone they know about it. Your mate is one of God's greatest blessings to you. Make sure other people know of your regard for your beloved. Don't keep your beloved's good qualities a secret. Speak of your blessings to others.

"And all nations will call you blessed,
for you will be a delightful land,"
says the LORD of hosts.

Malachi 3:12

Liberation

Love liberates. It can give you both wings to fly and a place to stand. Seek to give your mate courage and the space to grow into all that God has designed him or her to be. Live a life of love, and it will set you free.

And I will walk at liberty,
for I seek Your precepts.

Psalm 119:45

Seeking

*L*ife can seem like a series of closed doors. Don't be afraid to ask to have the doors opened. God wants you and your beloved to seek what you want—you will find it. That is His generous promise to you.

The heart of the prudent acquires knowledge, and the ear of the wise seeks knowledge.

Proverbs 18:15

Focus

*F*ocus your heart on the heart of God, and He will work miracles in your love life. Seek to follow God's example as you relate to your loved one. He will bless you as your minds and hearts are stayed on Him.

God, my heart is steady.
I will sing and praise you
with all my being.

Psalm 108:1 NCV

Sweetness

*L*et your mind savor sweetness, whether it is a sweet thought of your beloved or a sweet moment with the Lord. Soak your being in love, and let affection be the hallmark that describes your life.

The wise in heart will be called
prudent, and sweetness of the
lips increases learning.

Proverbs 16:21

Transparency

When you truly love and are loved by someone, there is little need for secrets. After all, most of your faults and shortcomings are already known to the other. The good news is that those in love *accept each other anyway.*

He reveals deep and secret things;
He knows what is in the darkness,
and light dwells with Him.

Daniel 2:22

Worth

God is the surgeon who sees the wounds—large or small—in our spirits and can make them well. He sees what we seek to hide, and He knows the worth of our love for others. Let God today be the surgeon in your lives. Let Him do whatever is necessary to make you whole.

All the ways of a man are
pure in his own eyes, but the
LORD weighs the spirits.

Proverbs 16:2

Alongside

*I*f inner troubles plague your marriage, don't give up. The One who has borne all your transgressions is also the One who gives you hope for a new tomorrow. He walks alongside you and your mate. He will never abandon you or leave you comfortless. That's His promise to you. Believe it. Live your life *knowing it is true.*

***

Surely He has borne our griefs
and carried our sorrows.

Isaiah 53:4

Glory

Think about our Lord's birth in a manger. Sing praises to God for the wondrous way in which He showed His endless love to all of humankind. Be thankful for the gift of a mate who loves and cares about this priceless gift.

Glory to God in the highest,
and on earth peace,
goodwill toward men!

Luke 2:14

Miracle

Reflect on the miracle of Jesus' birth, and ask Him to continue the miracle of love He has begun inside of you. Renew your vows with your mate. Let this day be one of joy, fulfillment, and hope.

And you will have joy and gladness,
and many will rejoice at his birth.

Luke 1:14

Despair

Despair is only for a span of time. God can bring your heart to a place of rejoicing and gladness. Thank Him for the care He gives to all of His children. The four most comforting words in the English language are: *this too shall pass.* Don't despair . . . joy comes in the morning.

❧

Oh, satisfy us early with Your
mercy, that we may rejoice
and be glad all our days!

Psalm 90:14

Sanctuary

ake of your love a safe sanctuary for you and your beloved. Keep your relationship with your mate healthy and strong so it may be a place of comfort and retreat from the troubles of life.

And He brought them to His
holy border, this mountain which
His right hand had acquired.

Psalm 78:54

Image

Do not conform to the image of the world in your marriage. Spend time in God's Word, and learn to love as God has loved. Be patient with your spouse, and nurture your mate as God would. See that your values reflect those of the Father.

And do not be conformed to this
world, but be transformed by the
renewing of your mind, that you
may prove what is that good and
acceptable and perfect will of God.

Romans 12:2

Hope

Hope is a defense against many troubles in your life. Exercise hope as you talk with your mate. Pray in faith, believing that God will answer your prayers. Ground your hope in His love.

Remember the word to Your
servant, upon which You
have caused me to hope.

Psalm 119:49

Consider

Consider the ways in which God has guided you and blessed your family. Pray with your beloved for God to direct your path each day of the year. May God grant to you and your mate His very best this day . . . and every day to come.

I thought about my ways,
and turned my feet to
Your testimonies.

Psalm 119:59

Facing
Hard Times

Fortress

Love is a fortress against troubles from all sides. It will withstand fierce storms if your relationship is sturdy and strong. Be strong together.

Better is a dinner of herbs where love is,
than a fatted calf with hatred.

Proverbs 15:17

Oneness

evelop a sense of oneness with your partner. Use disagreements to build your relationship by talking about problems when they occur. Don't let resentment build a wall between you. If you do, it can become a wedge that can split you apart.

"And if a house is divided against itself, that house cannot stand."

Mark 3:25

Calm

*I*f you feel overwhelmed by the storms in your relationship with your beloved, don't despair. Ask God to come into the midst of your problems and bring you His calm and all-abiding peace to strengthen your togetherness.

But He said to them, "Why are you fearful, O you of little faith?" Then He arose and rebuked the winds and the sea, and there was a great calm.

Matthew 8:26

Runs Over

Give to your beloved until the cup runs over. Don't wait to receive from your loved one before *you* show your love. When your beloved is disappointed by life and its cares, give your lover even more love and support.

But Elkanah always gave a special
share of the meat to Hannah,
because he loved Hannah and
because the LORD had kept
her from having children.

1 Samuel 1:5 NCV

Consideration

Make sure your actions match your words. Don't tell someone, "I love you. Oh, how I love you," and then neglect to show him or her love in action and deed. Be kind and considerate with your loved one.

I may speak in different languages
of people or even angels. But if
I do not have love, I am only a
noisy bell or a crashing cymbal.

1 Corinthians 13:1 NCV

Commit

Commit yourself to the promises of God in the hard times. Don't give way to a bottomless pit of despair. Talk to God about your feelings. Remind Him of the promises He has made to His people—to *you*!

Blessed is the man who endures temptation; for when he has been approved, he will receive the crown of life which the Lord has promised to those who love Him.

James 1:12

Love

Don't underestimate the power of love to see you through the hard times. Faith and hope are vital. But the Bible tells us that love continues to win the day. Tell your mate of your love even more when the hard times come.

And now abide faith, hope, love, these three; but the greatest of these is love.

1 Corinthians 13:13

Quietness

*B*e grateful for these times with your mate that are filled with richness, quietness, and contentment. Don't let the pursuit of money or fame become a substitute for spending time nourishing your love relationship.

In returning and rest you shall be saved;
in quietness and confidence
shall be your strength.

Isaiah 30:15

Positive

Look for times in your love relationship when you can speak a word of encouragement or praise. Don't hesitate to tell of the joy you enjoy with your loved one. Positive words strengthen the bond of love you share.

People enjoy giving good advice.
Saying the right word at the
right time is so pleasing.

Proverbs 15:23 NCV

No Hiding

Don't be misled. Adultery can never be hidden. The effects show in your life, and your mate will know of your betrayal, even if it's only in the guilt you are trying to hide.

You cannot carry hot coals against
your chest without burning your
clothes. . . . The same is true if
you have sexual relations with
another man's wife. Anyone who
does so will be punished.

Proverbs 6:27, 29 NCV

Enemies

Remember, you don't have to face your troubles alone. God is on the side of His children, and He will stand with you as you face the obstacles in your life. Nor are you alone in your physical relationship. Stand strong with your beloved.

But we can win with God's help.
He will defeat our enemies.

Psalm 108:13 NCV

Strife

*S*eek to find peace in the troubles and challenges of your relationship. Remember, love is not a contest; it is an exciting, cooperative venture that explores the uncharted worlds of relationship. Blessed is the one who makes peace.

It is honorable for a man to
stop striving, since any fool
can start a quarrel.

Proverbs 20:3

Secrets

Be careful about having secrets from your mate. Learn to be open and vulnerable. Openness develops trust and trust builds love. Ask God for courage to be *transparently you* with the one you love.

Stolen water is sweet,
and bread eaten in secret is pleasant.
But he does not know that the
dead are there, that her guests
are in the depths of hell.

Proverbs 9:17–18

Boldly

Come to God boldly. Ask Him what you need in your relationship with your beloved. The path of love will at times be rough indeed. Ask God to help you smooth the way. All you have to do is ask.

Let us therefore come boldly
to the throne of grace, that
we may obtain mercy and find
grace to help in time of need.

Hebrews 4:16

Frustration

Being angry is not a sin. However, be careful that your anger does not lead you to sin. Talk about your fears, frustrations, and hurts with your beloved. Don't hold your anger inside.

"Be angry, and do not sin": do not let the sun go down on your wrath.

Ephesians 4:26

Tenderness

True love outlasts the most difficult of times. Nourish your love in the hard times. It will make your troubles more bearable. Learn to stand close to your beloved when storms shake your household.

Love never fails.

1 Corinthians 13:8

Losses

God replaces your losses with good things. If you are following Him and lose someone close to you, always remember how much He cares and that He has promised to fill your aching void with His special kind of love.

So Jesus answered and said,
"Assuredly, I say to you, there is no
one who has left house or brothers
or sisters or father or mother or wife
or children or lands, for My sake and
the gospel's, who shall not receive
a hundredfold now in this time."

Mark 10:29–30

Wise One

True love doesn't just happen. It's God who gives us the power to love. If you find it difficult to express love, ask God for His direction and insight. He will give you the ability and the wisdom to love better and stronger than you ever dreamed possible.

He who does not love does not
know God, for God is love.

1 John 4:8

Destruction

Don't fool yourself. If you commit adultery, you are doing more than just harming the relationship you share with your mate. You may be irreparably damaging your very soul. The guilt and deceit can eat away at your conscience until you are consumed.

Whoever commits adultery with a woman lacks understanding; he who does so destroys his own soul.

Proverbs 6:32

Relish

Learn to be joyful and relish the love you have with your mate. Don't let troubles rob you of an exuberant happiness in being together. Hug your lover, and talk of your special feelings. Do it right now! Do it often!

Enjoy life with the wife you love.

Ecclesiastes 9:9 NCV

Shade

When it seems like your troubles beat against you relentlessly, remember God has promised to be your shade. He has promised to refresh you in the battles you face and to keep you.

The LORD is your keeper;
the LORD is your shade
at your right hand.

Psalm 121:5

Never Alone

*I*f you have problems, don't wait to take them to God. You cannot face your hard times alone. Ask God to intervene and give you wisdom. He will stand with you in each situation. Better yet, together—you and your mate—take your problems and concerns to the Lord in earnest prayer.

They wandered in the wilderness in a desolate way; they found no city to dwell in. . . . Then they cried out to the LORD in their trouble, and He delivered them out of their distresses.

Psalm 107:4, 6

Worries

If you and your mate are afraid or nervous, remember that God has promised to send His angels and His Holy Spirit to watch over you. Do not worry; God is in charge and He loves you both more than you'll ever know.

For He shall give His angels charge over you, to keep you in all your ways.

Psalm 91:11

Dreams

*G*od specializes in new beginnings for couples. Throughout history and in the present, God has given new dreams to couples and has stood with them as their most cherished dreams came true. Don't be afraid to ask God for a new plan for your future.

Then God said to Abraham, "As for Sarai your wife, you shall not call her name Sarai, but Sarah shall be her name. And I will bless her and also give you a son by her; then I will bless her, and she shall be a mother of nations; kings of peoples shall be from her."

Genesis 17:15–16

Sacrifices

Don't be a martyr to your mate. Give from a joyful heart and not as one who is forced to make sacrifices. Remember that true, abiding love comes from the heart, not from the bank account.

Better is a dry morsel with quietness,
than a house full of feasting with strife.

Proverbs 17:1

Returning

*I*f it's been a while since you and your mate have turned to God and really listened to Him, don't despair. It's never too late for the repentant heart to seek His face. Do it together. Call on Him today.

Restore us, O God;
cause Your face to shine,
and we shall be saved!

Psalm 80:3

Honesty

When you and your mate come before God, don't pretend you are satisfied when you are not. Talk over any misunderstandings you may have with one another. God longs for honesty from His people who want to get to know Him more completely.

For He satisfies the longing soul,
and fills the hungry soul
with goodness.

Psalm 107:9

Strength

When you are facing hard times, don't worry if you seem to be weak and helpless. God promises to give you His strength to do what you need to do. Pray to your loving Father, and ask Him to bring strength to your weakness.

By You I have been upheld from birth; You are He who took me out of my mother's womb. My praise shall be continually of You.

Psalm 71:6

Grief

When you grieve, it's all right to weep. But don't weep as those couples who have no hope. The God of all creation listens to you when you mourn, and He has promised to comfort you and bless you with good things.

He who continually goes forth
weeping, bearing seed for
sowing, shall doubtless come
again with rejoicing, bringing
his sheaves with him.

Psalm 126:6

Growing
with God

Blissful

Go to bed tonight with blissful thoughts of what God has done and is doing in your marriage and in your family life. Give thanks to Him and to your spouse for the happiness you are enjoying each day. Praise Him for your love together.

The words of the pure are pleasant.

Proverbs 15:26

Vulnerable

*H*onesty is one of the most vital ingredients in a loving relationship. If you are afraid of being fully known by your beloved, practice by first being vulnerable before God. Share deeply with Him. Tell Him things unknown to others. Once you feel His boundless acceptance, you'll find yourself better prepared to be honest with your beloved.

Search me, O God, and know my heart;
try me, and know my anxieties.

Psalm 139:23

Revenge

When you feel hurt or unloved, you may want to hit back. In your heart, you know that revenge doesn't build love. Talk about your hurts and disappointments with your beloved. Love your spouse today as never before.

Beloved, do not avenge yourselves,
but rather give place to wrath; for
it is written, "Vengeance is Mine,
I will repay," says the Lord.

Romans 12:19

Cuddle

Does your beloved seem far away, lost in concerns and problems? Everyone feels alone at times—uncared for and seemingly without a friend. Remember, that's one of the best times to draw nigh to God. Literally *see yourself cuddling in His arms*. He is your friend and constant companion. Then take that spirit of God's love and share it with your mate. Enjoy an evening of cuddling . . . *of just being together.*

Come near to God, and God
will come near to you.

James 4:8 NCV

Devotions

Set aside a regular time to read God's Word with your beloved. As your souls grow closer to the soul of God, you will find yourselves growing closer to each other. Make *shared devotions* once a day a vital part of your relationship and your spiritual growth together.

"You search the Scriptures, for in them you think you have eternal life; and these are they which testify of Me."

John 5:39

Pleasures

*R*ejoice in the pleasures God has given to you in your marriage. Thank Him for the abundance of affection and passion with which He has blessed you. Remember how He smiles when you drink deeply of His gifts.

They are abundantly satisfied
with the fullness of Your house,
and You give them drink from
the river of Your pleasures.

Psalm 36:8

Comprehension

*I*f you wish you had greater comprehension of your beloved, yourself, and others, don't despair. God has promised His boundless wisdom to those who come to Him in faith—believing. Ask God to open your eyes. In so doing, you'll be like the blind man in the Bible who simply said, "Once I was blind, but now I can see." Ask God for that sight—and insight—today.

Open my eyes, that I may see
wondrous things from Your law.

Psalm 119:18

Loving-Kindness

Keep your eyes focused on the positive, good things in your love relationship— the qualities that brought you together in the first place. Look for ways to compliment your beloved. A single word of praise does more good than pages of well-meant criticism.

For Your lovingkindness is before my eyes,
and I have walked in Your truth.

Psalm 26:3

Loyalty

The loyalty you feel for your beloved is precious beyond words. Tell your mate that you will "stand fast" all the way. It's easy to be gracious when you're riding the crest of personal success. Be there for the hard times too.

But Ruth said, "Don't beg me to leave you or to stop following you. Where you go, I will go. Where you live, I will live. Your people will be my people, and your God will be my God."

Ruth 1:16 NCV

Laughter

*L*augh joyously with your beloved. Lift your eyes to the sky, and praise God for the light He has given you in your love life together. He directs you in plentiful paths. Walk them with joy and gladness.

Light shines on those who do right;
joy belongs to those who are honest.

Psalm 97:11 NCV

Openness

Speak your emotions freely. Your love will flourish as a result of the outpouring of your heart. The same is true in your relationship with God. He wants you to tell Him how you feel. Speak your mind. Share your heart. God will listen and comfort you in all yours ways.

Lord, I call to you with all my heart. Answer me, and I will keep your demands.

Psalm 119:145 NCV

Fruits

Seek to love your mate with all the fruits of the Spirit. Let your relationship be a model for all others to see—especially if you have a child. If you lack any of the fruits, ask the One who gives abundantly to all who seek. Our God is loving and generous. Ask and you will receive.

But the Spirit produces the fruit of love, joy, peace, patience, kindness, goodness, faithfulness, gentleness, self-control. There is no law that says these things are wrong.

Galatians 5:22–23 NCV

Choice

You can't earn love; love is a gift. You can't buy love; it's simply not for sale. And that's especially true for God's love. God gives us love because He has chosen to do so. No one has ever been good enough or rich enough to earn His love. So it is with your spouse. No one is ever good enough to receive love. We love *simply because we choose to love*. Unconditional love is the most powerful force on earth.

He took me to a safe place.
Because he delights in
me, he saved me.

Psalm 18:19

No Regret

If you have a love thought for your beloved, speak it now! There are no guarantees from day to day. Take the time today to express your love. Live today with your love as though this were the last.

All flesh is as grass, and all the
glory of man as the flower of the
grass. The grass withers, and its
flower falls away, but the word
of the LORD endures forever.

1 Peter 1:24–25

Equals

The Bible says we are all equally precious in the eyes of God. Put your beloved's concerns on an equal footing with your own. Search for the best in your spouse. In so doing, your love relationship will flourish. Enjoy the dream of staying in love—*forever*.

There is neither Jew nor Greek,
there is neither slave nor free, there
is neither male nor female; for
you are all one in Christ Jesus.

Galatians 3:28

Reflections

*S*hare your deepest reflections with your beloved. Talk often of the things on your mind and on your heart. The more you share, the closer you'll come to each other in love and understanding. Give the one you love the gift of yourself.

How precious also are Your
thoughts to me, O God!
How great is the sum of them!

Psalm 139:17

Conceitedness

Conceitedness is a dangerous ingredient in a love relationship. You're walking on egg-shells when you begin to feel you are the only one who knows or understands the situation. Chances are, you'll soon find yourself alone with your store of knowledge. Always look at both sides of the issue. It still takes two to tango.

There is more hope for a
foolish person than for those
who think they are wise.

Proverbs 26:12 NCV

Blossom

*L*ove your spouse, and ask God to make your love blossom into a tree that shades your life together with goodness and contentment. Do not count the cost of love; look only to the end result of your togetherness.

So Boaz took Ruth and she became his wife; and when he went in to her, the LORD gave her conception, and she bore a son.

Ruth 4:13

Waiting

Pray for your love relationship with the confidence that God will give you the desires of your heart. God listens to your pleas and deepest concerns. His ears are waiting to hear your inner desires. He cares about you and your beloved.

For the eyes of the LORD are on the righteous, and His ears are open to their prayers; but the face of the LORD is against those who do evil.

1 Peter 3:12

Togetherness

he Bible says that the harmony of your love life affects the working of your prayers. God does not respond to your supplications in the same way if you pray from one side of your mouth while fighting with your mate out of the other. Let your life together be one in harmony.

❧

In the same way, you husbands should live with your wives in an understanding way, since they are weaker than you. But show them respect, because God gives them the same blessing he gives you—the grace that gives true life. Do this so that nothing will stop your prayers.

1 Peter 3:7 NCV

Build Up

*B*uild up your beloved in the faith of our Lord, Jesus Christ. Encourage your mate with prayer and the witness of what God has done in your own life. Together grow in the knowledge of Him, His love, and His goodness.

But dear friends, use your most holy faith to build yourselves up, praying in the Holy Spirit. Keep yourselves in God's love as you wait for the Lord Jesus Christ with his mercy to give you life forever.

Jude vv. 20–21 ncv

Meditate

Study the Scriptures. Meditate on God's Word. Read His promises together with your beloved, and talk about what His divine counsel means in your everyday life. The Bible is as fresh today as when it was first given to humankind. Let it be your guide in your own loving relationship with your spouse.

＊

The LORD's words are pure,
like silver purified by fire,
like silver purified seven times over.

Psalm 12:6 NCV

Growth

The farmer is not allowed to have a harvest the day after planting. A good crop takes time, patience, and tender loving care. It's akin to your relationship with your spouse. God is working to draw you and your beloved closer together *and to Him.*

"I tell you the truth, a grain of wheat must fall to the ground and die to make many seeds. But if it never dies, it remains only a single seed."

John 12:24 NCV

Witnessing

By your example of love and caring, love your unbelieving mate into a relationship with God. Intrigue your spouse with words consistent with your loving actions. Show your beloved what a difference God continues to make in your own life. Love your mate into embracing the Gospel.

❧

After some days Felix came with his wife, Drusilla, who was Jewish, and asked for Paul to be brought to him. He listened to Paul talk about believing in Christ Jesus.

Acts 24:24 NCV

Success

Celebrate every success with your mate. Lift your arms and give thanks. Embrace the peaks of joy and happiness. God is in all good things. Applaud your mate's achievements with enthusiasm. Join together in thanksgiving.

David went back to bless the people in his home, but Saul's daughter Michal came out to meet him. She said, "With what honor the king of Israel acted today! You took off your clothes in front of the servant girls of your officers like one who takes off his clothes without shame!"

2 Samuel 6:20 ɴᴄᴠ

Beginnings

The beginnings of love are like a vapor. There may be times when it seems easier to just let it blow away. But God puts His angels before you and desires to stop the vapor from disappearing. Ask Him to keep your love alive. He wants the best for the two of you as you continue to share your life living and loving together.

The angel of the LORD
encamps all around those who
fear Him, and delivers them.

Psalm 34:7

Jewel

Treat your love like a precious jewel. Gaze at the sparkling stone, but do not smash it to see how it's been created. Leave some room for mystery. Let your love be a constant unraveling of the good things between you.

Delilah said to Samson, "Until now you have mocked me and told me lies. . . ." And it came to pass, when she pestered him daily with her words and pressed him, so that his soul was vexed to death, that he told her all his heart.

Judges 16:13, 16–17

Comfort

*G*od binds up the rejected. If your beloved turns from you, know that you will be comforted in the arms of your heavenly Father. He grieves with those who grieve, and He comforts all who turn to Him. Rejection is painful. But whatever does not kill you *makes you stronger.*

"For the LORD has called you like
a woman forsaken and grieved in
spirit, like a youthful wife when you
were refused," says your God.

Isaiah 54:6

Anticipation

God will always welcome you with open arms. No request is too small or too big to bring to Him. Tell our gracious Lord all that is on your heart regarding the one you love. Learn to pray for that which is difficult. While praying, anticipate God doing the impossible.

Jesus turned and saw the woman and said, "Be encouraged, dear woman. You are made well because you believed." And the woman was healed from that moment on.

Matthew 9:22 NCV

Rejoicing in Abundance

Growing

The Lord of all the heavens and earth has blessed you with His love and care. He delights in pleasing you throughout your days and in helping you and your beloved grow to full stature.

I will sing to the LORD, because He has dealt bountifully with me.

Psalm 13:6

Overflowing

*G*ive and it shall be given back to you, pressed down and overflowing. An open heart and a gentle, open hand are the best assurances of a long and lasting love affair with your mate.

Whoever gives to others will get
richer; those who help others
will themselves be helped.

Proverbs 11:25 NCV

Anointing

God rains down His anointing power on His people. If you or your spouse has any lack, go to the Father who knows your every need. He will open His great storehouses of blessings and shower you with His generous heart.

You prepare a meal for me
in front of my enemies.
You pour oil of blessing on my head;
you fill my cup to overflowing.
Surely your goodness and love will
be with me all my life, and I will live
in the house of the LORD forever.

Psalm 23:5–6 NCV

Smile

A smile can warm the coldest heart. Think on good things, and your smile will radiate a contentment that will draw others to you. Adding more smiles to your marriage inevitably adds more romance to your life.

A happy heart is like good
medicine, but a broken spirit
drains your strength.

Proverbs 17:22

Gifts

*I*f you and your spouse were to count all the wondrous things God has done for you, you would soon be overwhelmed. He gave you life and sustenance and continues to share with you His all-abiding love. He also gave you a mind and a heart to appreciate all He has given.

All of you who fear God, come
and listen, and I will tell you
what he has done for me.

Psalm 66:16 NCV

Hang On

Get a grip on hope, and hang on tight. Hope is the cable that rescues us from despair and lethargy. Hang on tight and keep expecting God to work a miracle in your life.

But I will always have hope
and will praise you more and more.

Psalm 71:14 ncv

Praise

Compliments bring a sparkle to everyone's eyes. Be a person who looks for reasons to compliment your beloved. Notice the fabric of your spouse's personality, and give all the encouragement and praise you can.

The light of the eyes rejoices
the heart, and a good report
makes the bones healthy.

Proverbs 15:30

Creation

God's hand flung the moon into space and set the sun in its orbit. He holds the stars in His power and moves the seas at His whim. Rejoice in the special love He has created for you and your beloved.

Both the day and the night are yours;
you made the sun and the moon.

Psalm 74:16 NCV

Unmeasured

*L*ove your mate without restraint. Don't measure your love and weigh what you receive in return. Be a lover who gives yourself today with no thought for the hurts of the past or the problems of the future.

"Give, and it will be given to you:
good measure, pressed down,
shaken together, and running over
will be put into your bosom. For with
the same measure that you use, it
will be measured back to you."

Luke 6:38

Endurance

If you feel alone and insignificant, don't despair. God lifts up the humble and comforts those who are abandoned. Bring your heart to Him for healing and new hope.

But You, O Lord, shall endure
forever, and the remembrance of
Your name to all generations.

Psalm 102:12

Favor

God has put His loving hand on the pulse of your life, and He has given you wondrous gifts. Thank Him for the gift of love He has given to you through your special mate.

He who finds a wife finds a good thing,
and obtains favor from the LORD.

Proverbs 18:22

Enjoy!

Savor each day, and drink of its sweetness. Treasure each moment of vibrant life the Lord has given to you. Don't wile away your hours or days waiting for what will be. Enjoy what *is*. Do it now!

This is the day the LORD has made;
we will rejoice and be glad in it.

Psalm 118:24

Grace

God has spread His mantle of protection over your family. He loves the ones you love even more than you do. Come to Him as a family, and ask for the grace you each need to live out your days.

May the LORD give you increase more and more, you and your children.

Psalm 115:14

Prosper

Lift your arms to the sky, and thank God for the sunshine He has given to you. Every ounce of energy you have has been given to you by Him. Rejoice in the abundance of health and wealth He has given you and your beloved.

Beloved, I pray that you may
prosper in all things and be in
health, just as your soul prospers.

3 John v. 2

Satiated

Your words of love are a sweet nectar to your beloved. Pour love words on the heart of your mate until you are both satiated. Celebrate your love and be enormously happy together.

How sweet are Your words
to my taste, sweeter than
honey to my mouth!

Psalm 119:103

Testimonies

God has woven threads of gold throughout your life. Don't hesitate to remind yourself and others of the good things God has done for you in the past. It gives you reason to hope. Explore the good of days gone by . . . enjoy your past heritage and share it with others.

Your testimonies I have taken
as a heritage forever, for they
are the rejoicing of my heart.

Psalm 119:111

Honor

Crown your life with honor. Be careful that scandal doesn't rightfully attach to your name. Live your life honestly, and you and your beloved will enjoy peace in all your dealings.

My brothers and sisters, above all, do not use an oath when you make a promise. Don't use the name of heaven, earth, or anything else to prove what you say. When you mean yes, say only yes, and when you mean no, say only no so you will not be judged guilty.

James 5:12 ncv

Delight

*P*our warm laughter over your life with your beloved. Ask the Father who delights in each of us to teach you to delight in the ways of each other as children delight in each new day's discoveries.

He also brought me out into a
broad place; He delivered me
because He delighted in me.

2 Samuel 22:20

Priceless

Love is a great treasure hunt. Seek to discover the priceless and special facets of your beloved's heart and soul. One way to discover the treasures of your spouse is to read God's Word together and meditate on His love.

I rejoice at Your word as one
who finds great treasure.

Psalm 119:162

Emotional

*L*ove your mate with an active, emotional love. Hear the joys and the sadness of the one you love. Remind your beloved of your steadfast love during challenging times of your life.

Her husband Elkanah would say
to her, "Hannah, why are you
crying and why won't you eat?
Why are you sad? Don't I mean
more to you than ten sons?"

1 Samuel 1:8 NCV

Refresh

*R*efresh yourself with the love you share with your heart's partner. Shape your love into the same kind of love God gives to each of you. May your affection be a shade tree during life's dry seasons.

The LORD is your keeper; the LORD
is your shade at your right hand.
The sun shall not strike you by
day, nor the moon by night.

Psalm 121:5–6

Soul

*F*eel the texture of your beloved's spirit. Spend time together in prayer so you know the soul of your mate as well as you know your own. It takes time . . . but you will be richer as a result of your caring.

"And do not fear those who kill
the body but cannot kill the soul.
But rather fear Him who is able to
destroy both soul and body in hell."

Matthew 10:28

Thankful

Develop a thankful heart. Look for reasons to be thankful to God and to your mate. A thankful tongue will water your relationship until love blossoms beyond your greatest expectations.

Let the heavens rejoice,
and let the earth be glad.
Let the sea roar, and all its fullness.

Psalm 96:11

Perspective

Offer criticism cautiously. In any relationship, there are two sides to every issue. Examine your own actions before you turn a critical eye to the actions of your mate. Your task is to love, not criticize. If you need to change your perspective, start changing today, not tomorrow.

❧

"And why do you look at the speck in your brother's eye, but do not perceive the plank in your own eye?"

Luke 6:41

Forgiveness

orgiveness can make the sun shine on a marriage in trouble. It will make love sprout and grow in ground that once seemed barren. Don't bear grudges against your beloved. Freely forgive.

For You, Lord, are good, and ready
to forgive, and abundant in mercy
to all those who call upon You.

Psalm 86:5

Troubles

The ongoing challenges of life can place heavy burdens of you and your mate. Learn to lift the weight together so the troubles do not crush either of you. Almost any burden, when shared equally, can be borne. Flex your muscles together. The load will be lighter.

The workers help each other and
say to each other, "Be strong!"

Isaiah 41:6 NCV

Gratitude

*G*ive praise unto God. Hold hands with your beloved, and stand before the Almighty in gratitude for who He is and what He has done in your own private world. Keep your eyes focused on Him, and He will give you a peace beyond understanding.

I will praise You, O LORD, with
my whole heart; I will tell of
all Your marvelous works.

Psalm 9:1

Brightness

*L*oneliness is a dark place. Emptiness seems to surround you. Then your beloved enters. The love of your spouse is a bright and glowing candle that lights every corner of your solitary existence.

The Son reflects the glory of God and shows exactly what God is like. He holds everything together with his powerful word. When the Son made people clean from their sins, he sat down at the right side of God, the Great One in heaven.

Hebrews 1:3 NCV

Little Things

Little phrases like, "Please forgive," or, "I care," will make a big difference in your marriage. Don't neglect the seemingly *little* words; they speak richly of your special love and attention.

A word fitly spoken is like apples
of gold in settings of silver.

Proverbs 25:11

Building
a Family

Children

If you yearn for children and have none of your own, come to God in prayer. God delights in giving you good things. Ask Him to bless you with a child to love and to cherish.

He gives children to the woman who has none and makes her a happy mother. Praise the LORD!

Psalm 113:9 NCV

Example

If you want your children to grow to be God-fearing men and women, then you and your mate need to show them how God-fearing people live. There is no substitute for a loving example. Be that example of God's love today.

Praise the LORD! Blessed is the man who fears the LORD, who delights greatly in His commandments.

Psalm 112:1

Law

It is important to teach your children the law and the love of God. Read the Scriptures *together* as a family. Give your kids the chance to ask questions about your beliefs. Say in words *they can understand* what God has done in the lives of you and your mate.

My son, hear the instruction of your
father, and do not forsake the law
of your mother; for they will be a
graceful ornament on your head,
and chains about your neck.

Proverbs 1:8–9

Discipline

Discipline is a difficult area for many families. Discuss with your mate how you both wish to deal with the various areas of challenge in raising children. Then be both firm and compassionate in your daily discipline—always speaking the truth in love.

For whom the LORD loves He corrects, just as a father the son in whom he delights.

Proverbs 3:12

Training

Have hope as you nurture your children. The Bible says the early training will abide with them, even when they are old. Make it a happy habit to talk with your children at an early age about God's love.

Train up a child in the way he
should go, and when he is old
he will not depart from it.

Proverbs 22:6

Faith

Faith is contagious. When you and your spouse speak of your faith and live it in your everyday lives, your children will be influenced by its power. Show your kids how to have faith today.

I remember your true faith. That faith
first lived in your grandmother Lois
and in your mother Eunice, and I
know you now have that same faith.

2 Timothy 1:5 NCV

Truth

each your children to tell the truth. A respect for honesty will serve them well throughout their entire lives. Be sure to speak the truth yourself in your dealings with others. Your kids will see it and follow your example.

Nothing gives me greater joy
than to hear that my children are
following the way of truth.

3 John v. 4 NCV

Gentleness

*G*uide your children with gentleness and kindness. Show them kindness from an early age, and train them with a godly affection. Even when you must discipline, be sure your children know that they are loved *simply for who they are.*

Even though as apostles of Christ
we could have used our authority
over you. But we were very
gentle with you, like a mother
caring for her little children.

1 Thessalonians 2:7 NCV

Obedience

each your children to obey you. Early lessons in respect for authority provide them with a firm base for success in relationships with others. When you are affectionate with your children, it is easier for them to want to do what you say.

Children, obey your parents in
the Lord, for this is right.

Ephesians 6:1

Rebellion

on't be so stern with your children that you cause them to be angry and rebellious. Make every possible effort to be fair and just in your rules and expectations, and always handle your discipline with love.

Fathers, do not nag your children.
If you are too hard to please,
they may want to stop trying.

Colossians 3:21

Wisdom

When you train your child well, you will bear pleasant fruit in later years. A wise and righteous child will bring joy to the hearts of your and your spouse. Encourage your child in the ways of wisdom.

The father of a good child is very happy;
parents who have wise children
are glad because of them.

Proverbs 23:24 NCV

Eternal Soul

The soul of your children is a precious trust from the Lord. God wants each of His children to come to know Him. Teach your kids of God's love, and pray for their eternal salvation.

"Even so it is not the will of your Father who is in heaven that one of these little ones should perish."

Matthew 18:14

Legacy

Leave a legacy for your children. When you have children, you immediately begin to care more deeply about the care and feeding of the nation and the physical world. Talk with your spouse about what you two can do to help make our planet a better place for your kids to live.

One generation shall praise
Your works to another, and shall
declare Your mighty acts.

Psalm 145:4

Enthusiasm

on't underestimate your children. The natural dependency and openness of a child is so precious that Jesus said it was *child-like people who made up His kingdom*. Encourage your children to keep the enthusiasm of their early days—so that it may serve them well as they grow into adults.

＊

But Jesus said, "Let the little children come to Me, and do not forbid them; for of such is the kingdom of heaven."

Matthew 19:14

Champion

God is the champion of children. It is an honor to have Him give children into the care of you and your spouse. But He also stands with you as you struggle to raise your children.

"But whoever causes one of these
little ones who believe in Me to
stumble, it would be better for him if a
millstone were hung around his neck,
and he were thrown into the sea."

Mark 9:42

Covenant

God has made a commitment to you, your spouse, and your children. If you follow Him, He will remember you and redeem you. Be a gentle guide to your whole family as you yourself follow His counsel today.

He remembers His covenant forever,
the word which He commanded,
for a thousand generations.

Psalm 105:8

Heritage

Your children are a heritage from the Lord. He has placed them in your care to delight you and to challenge you to grow into the person He wants you to be.

Behold, children are a heritage
from the LORD, the fruit of
the womb is a reward.

Psalm 127:3

Instruction

*Y*our children are a blessing from God. He has given them to you for you to love and nurture. Show them the way of God's truth. Let your life and love point your children to the Lord.

My son, hear the instruction of
your father, and do not forsake
the law of your mother.

Proverbs 1:8

Family Resources Center
859 2287
(309) ~~637 1713~~